Brother Zone

Mary F McDonough

GADFLY

First edition published 5 December 2014
by Gadfly Editions

British Library Cataloguing in Publication Data
A CIP catalogue record for this book is
available from the British Library

ISBN 978-0-9928060-3-3

Designed and typeset in
Adobe Garamond Pro 9 / 11
by Martyn Clark

www.gadflyeditions.com
www.maryfmcdonough.com

For
Bren and Tristy
&
brothers
everywhere

PERSONAL NOTE

This book covers a year in the life of two brothers, aged five and seven, who love and fight with equal intensity. It's an exploration of how language is actually used in family life.

Until you have kids, it isn't really possible to understand how wonderful and terrible being a parent is. Nothing prepares you for the first tooth / word / steps, or for the first fratricidal moment of rage—the *'he started it!'* that shatters the cozy domestic dream.

We are natural and professional linguists—obsessed with words—and have always talked to the boys about them. In this book, we have tried to strike a balance between linguistics conventions and literary ones, so that we can better capture and present how we use language as a family in a way that's both rigorous and easy to read.

We're a mixed family: part Irish, British, and American, with a dash of Cherokee, French, Swiss, Japanese, Portuguese, Spanish and Italian thrown in. Lots of enchiladas, too.

And we're us.

Martyn & Mary

ACKNOWLEDGEMENTS

Thanks to Brendan and Tristan for giving us permission to publish this collection, and for allowing us to use their wonderful artwork. To Sophie Hayley, Helen MacKinven, Carolyn Dragon, Pauline Lindsay and Siobhan Hewison for proofreading, and to the many readers of the blog this collection started life as.

The production of this book was entirely funded by sales of The Last Pair of Ears. Thank you to everyone who has supported us along the way.

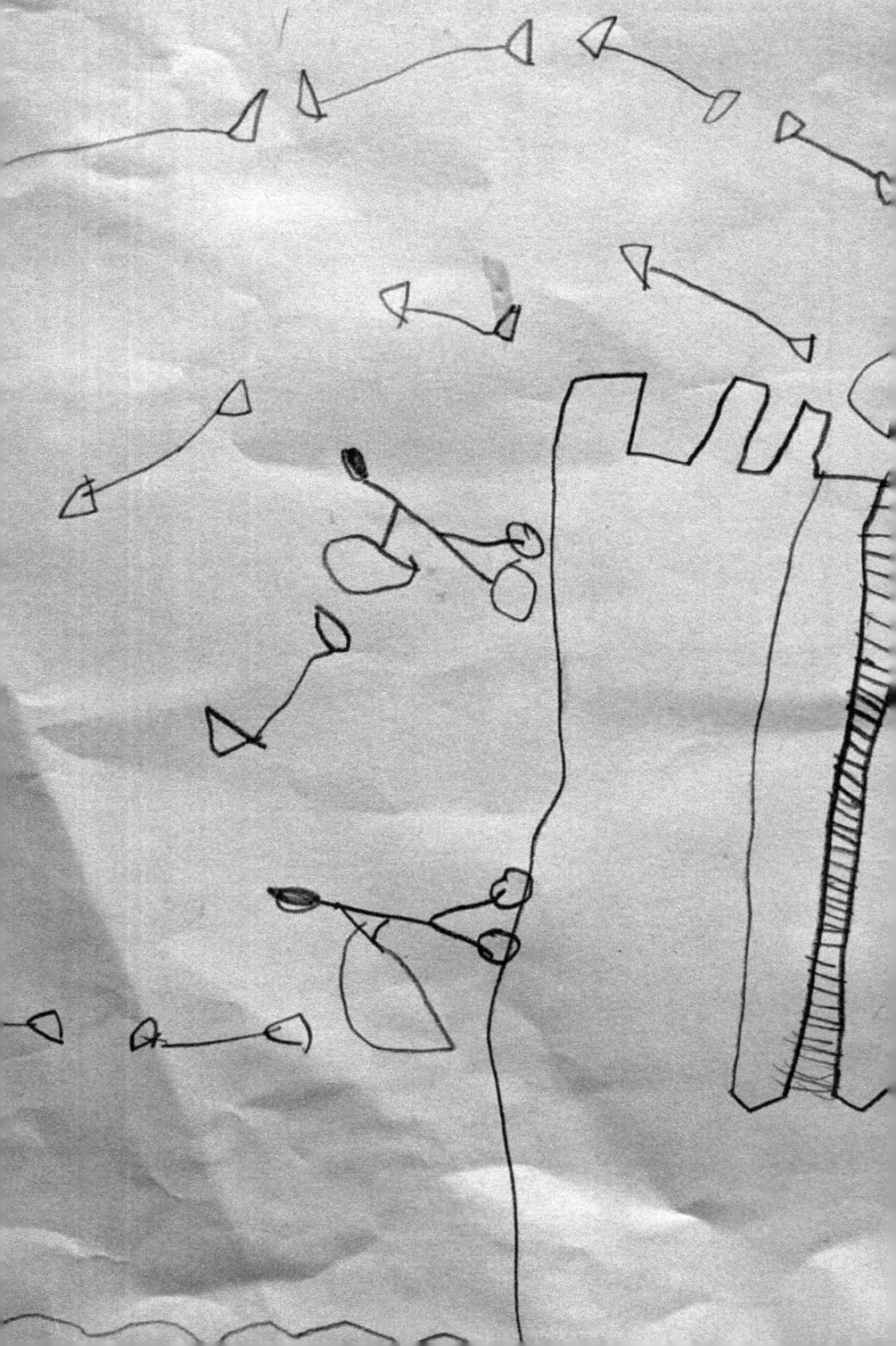

Hunched over their maps, two generals plan campaigns.
They arrange their armies. The rug is ruched and wrinkled
with great care. The terrain is mountainous, populated
with goats and flowers.

The generals agree, after 4 arguments and rolling the dice,
whose team is The Goodies: silent men, uniformly grey,
standing in long, grim, lines. The Goodies fight with
honor. The Baddies hide under covers, furniture, behind
the door. Virulent, poisonous, they have no scruples.

Wings flap. Bodies flail. Planes fall from the sky. Snakes
hiss. Men scream.

The Baddies, ably led by Medusa, several Decepticons, and
Polyphemus, defeat the modern warriors who bomb them
from stealth planes. Even the snipers, belatedly adopting
enemy tactics and hiding in the folds of the rug, are found
and eaten.

"Next time,"

shrieks General 1, stomping off,

"I'm being The Baddies!"

PETER PAWN AND TRANNY BELL

"I am NOT being a lady,
Brendan. You do Tinkerbell
AND Wendy! I have enough
guys to do!"

"You are only doing Peter Pan,
the Lost Boys, and Indians.
That's not too many parts."

"Well, I just don't want
to be a girl."

Tristan doesn't usually argue about assigned roles. He is happy to be anyone, as long as Brendan is willing to play with him. I think of him as Peter Pawn, the star of a play cursed, like Macbeth, which never goes according to plan, and always ends in actors walking off.

Brendan likes being Tranny Bell (as I now think of him) and Wendy. Swanning around in a black and silver dress, he is too distracted to continue the play. Jumping off the couch (trans.: flying over Neverland) is more fun when you are wearing sequins, and flecks of light bounce and scatter on the walls. Peter Pawn threatens to stab Tranny Bell if

"she doesn't just do what
she is supposed to do."

The play ends abruptly.

"If you can't control
your behaviour,

*Tristan, I am NOT
doing this show."*

Flounce, flounce, flourish: Peter Pawn is abandoned on-stage. Captain Hook—aka Big Cushion—soon buys it.

—Fin—

COFFEE

Brendan has gone skipping down the icy street to play
with a friend, ecstatic: Tristan has not been invited. Tristan
offers to make the coffee

> *"without spilling any of*
> *the beans"*

because

> *"you look thirsty*
> *and tired."*

I fall for it. I have a cold. Then,

> *"EEEEEW, Mom. This*
> *hot chocolate powder*
> *smells like cat litter."*

Hot chocolate? Who said anything about hot chocolate?
Turns out he wants to make me espresso with milk and
chocolate powder. I give in.

> *"EEEEW. This seriously*
> *smells like cat litter!"*

> *"Are you sure it smells*
> *like cat litter?"*

> *"Uh huh. It smells*
> *totally disgusting. I don't*
> *want to eat it out of the*
> *jar now."*

Aha! Now I know why I am being coerced into having choco-coffee.

> "Maybe…

[snidely]

> …*it is your breath you are*
> *smelling?*"

Tristan cups his hands, coughs into them, sniffs.

> > "Hey! It IS my breath that
> > smells vomity. I'm gonna
> > have some chocolate powder
> > after all. Thanks, Mom!"

I make the espresso myself. Tristan gloats about how angry Brendan is going to be when he

> > "gets back and I tell him you let me
> > eat LOADS of chocolate mix."

ELECTRIFYING DUMPLINGS

"Electrifying."

"What?"

*"You know… zzzz…
bzzz… zzzz,"*

with cheeks and eyes flicking from side to side.

*"It tastes sort of electrifying.
Which means zingy and not
too good. I don't think I like
soy sauce after all."*

BREAD MAN OF LEITH WALK

"Mom, can I choose the bread?
Can I use the pinchers? I'll race
you!"

I find him hanging from the shelf, tongue out, wrestling a
pistole with the tongs. He shouts, triumphantly waving
one small loaf:

"get a paper bag!"

Before I can open a bag, a man with white hair, bulging
eyes, and black NHS specs lunges past, grabs the last 3 rolls
out of the bin, and staggers away like Quasimodo, flour
covering his blue anorak.

"Did he just steal my bread, Mom?
That crazy Grandad just stealed
my bread!"

"I think he did, Tristy. We'll
have to choose something else."

"That guy was weird, Mom.
Is he from your hospital?"

"I don't know, honey.
Probably not."

"Can the police catch him?"

"No, not unless he didn't
pay, and runs over a cop on
his way out of here."

Birdwatching, trainspotting, bread-pinching, and other grown-up crimes are not strictly punishable. Tristan finds this odd. Bread is bread. He decides to choose some other bread, muttering

"freaks will go to jail if I am
in charge when I grow up."

I hope for Bread Man's sake that he is on his way to the airport.

CHINESE TEA TASTES LIKE WATER

Martyn made an attempt to get the conversation out of the *'yuk'* doldrums. The dumplings hadn't been a hit.

"Did you like your Chinese tea, Tristan?"

> *"Nope. It tasted just like water, only a bit more warmer."*

> *"What are those leaves floating in it, anyway?"*

Brendan, lifting the lid of the pot:

"That's the tea, Brendan. If you let it steep for a long time, it gets bitter, and I don't like it then."

Martyn, struggling in vain to raise the tone:

"I like it best just after they bring it to the table."

> *"I like the ice better, Dad, I can't resist it,"*

Tristan, chomping happily:

> *"it makes me have a chilly face and teeth."*

"And I like the hole in the middle. That is so cool! I've never seen ice cubes like this before. How did they make them? And, Dad, do people wait to make Chinese tea after the leaves are dead and rotten, or do they just look like this after they get boiled to death?"

Brendan is easily pleased and amazed.

"Next time, let's come by ourselves."

Martyn, sighing. I tell him to be quiet, and close his eyes; I am already imagining it.

"I'm floating! I'm floating! Look at my penis!! Floppy floating! Let's play the teacher game, Brendan! Fire in the hole! Farts in my bottom! My gas is…ungh… stinking up the room!"

"Miss! Look at my penis! Is it too floppy, teacher? Let's play the teacher at school game, and she has really bad kids in her class. But she likes that."

"Yeah! Awesome!"

"I like kids in my class being naughty. Guess how much water I have in my mouth, class?"

[spits water everywhere]

"This much!!"

"That was awesome, Brendan! Now it's my turn! Miss, Miss, I got some fish for you to eat. Take the wrapper off first."

[sniggering to himself]

*"Open up the bottomus of the
packet, miss! Farts in the hole!"*

"Tristan! Nipple ticklers!"

[spits water on Tristan's chest]

*"You are a total FREAK, Brendan,
and you annoy me!"*

*"I am so sorry. I simply must
trim your nipple hair. Pour
some water on them to take the
tickle out, Tristan."*

*"I'm fetchin' some maw water for
meself. I am spitting on you,
Brendan, and then I am telling!!
But first I am singing 'I've got a
hippopotamus under my bottomus
and my name is Otter-us!*

MOOOOOOOO-M!!"

MICROSOFT WORD

"Mom, I know what the 'W' picture means. It means Microsoft Word. It's for computers."

"How did you hear about Word, T?"

"At my school. I used it today."

"What did you do with Word?"

"I typed 'frogs are green.' It took me AGES."

TOO EARLY

"Ouch!! ARRRRGH! BRENDAN!
Put your torch back on! I can't see
Mom's side of the bed!! Spider is
hunting me! BREN... DAN!!!"

6:37 a.m. An hour before we need to get up. Starting the day with a scream and a cat with it's claws out really gets the fight-or-flight juices going. Tristan needs to go to the toilet. Brendan has agreed to escort him, but detours via my side of the bed, because

"I'm in the mood for love."

Martyn grumbles something about being in the mood for love too, but the bed is too damn crowded, and slouches off to the toilet.

Spider attacks anyone, other than me, who dares to approach *'Mom's bed'*—I spend so little time in it, I wonder why they refer to it that way. This includes Martyn. Tristan's fear of the dark has ratcheted up several thousand notches since Spider returned. He must really need to pee, if he is willing to risk being stalked. He admires Martyn:

"Dad is brave. He didn't even
take his iPhone to light the way."

Brendan officiously shines his torch in my face and

Tristan's, checking to make sure

"Spider isn't biting your throats."

Way to escalate, B. I am now blind, awake, and pretty sure, thanks to the adrenaline rush, that I will not be going back to sleep. Did I wake up in Guantanamo?

'Ooh! Mom! Up close, you look like a hologram, all dotty and stuff. My eyes aren't used to all of this light."

"Mine either, Tristan."

ONE BIG EYE

*"I know how they
made Bob."*

It is 8:41 a.m. My stupid grownup mind is focused on lots
of boring crap like pain, school bags, brushing teeth,
Spider legging it for the open door, and pain again. I try to
think like Tristan. I don't know which Bob he is talking
about. I scroll through a list of all possible Bobs, and
decide Tristan means BOB, from Monsters Versus Aliens.

I double-check, and he is quietly pleased that I have
caught up. He does a quick manly chin nod of agreement
that he must have been born knowing.

*"The Pixar guys made another
guy wear a blue suit and close
one of his eyes like this."*

He demonstrates, one eye held closed and the other one
opened with one grubby finger. I start thinking about
grownup stuff again—dirt, fingernails, must cut them before
judo this afternoon—but manage to stop myself in time.

This is a serious subject, almost sacred: one of the movies
in the pantheon he and Brendan have watched more than
20 times. I suggest that it might not have been a squinting
man in a blue suit, unless the Pixar guys filmed a blue suit
guy to copy his movements on the computer when they
were drawing BOB.

Tristan thinks about this, and decides it is possible that BOB

> *"was mostly drawn on computers,*
> *but I think it was probably a guy*
> *with only one giant eye, because*
> *doing this for a long time is sore."*

I look at his one blue eye that is open, his grubby hand
that is holding it open, and love him so much that I
almost can't breathe.

> *"I would like to meet a guy*
> *with one big eye like that."*

> *"Yeah! Me too! Unless it is*
> *Polyphemus. I would prefer to*
> *read about him than smell his*
> *dead-Greek breath."*

Amen, small man.

PENNIES

Brendan is always on the lookout for money.
Denomination doesn't matter. Currency isn't a
particularly big issue either, but he does prefer money
that he can spend

> *"today, if I get enough."*

Brendan sees grownups drop coins and not pick them up,
and wonders why they are so dumb.

> *"Do they not know it is real money,*
> *Mom, and if they save it, they will*
> *have more money?"*

I tell him that a lot of adults don't really seem to think of
small change as proper money. They prefer banknotes or
using a credit or debit card. Coins are heavy, and not
worth much. Some people also think it will make them
look poor or like they are stingy if they scrabble in the
gutter for 5 pence they've dropped.

> *"Well, when I see a penny, I think,*
> *WOW, I've only got to find 99 more,*
> *and then I will have a pound!"*

In Brendan's world, a penny is a downpayment on a future
dream he hasn't even had yet. He will be prepared for it
when it arrives, if he finds enough pennies.

GROWING UP IS BORING

"I want to be a spy when I grow up. But not ALL the time. I am going to be other stuff as well."

Tristan seems pretty sure about things. His list hasn't changed since he was two.

"Being a spy will be exciting. Sneaking around, weapons…"

A bit like his life now, then.

"It's gonna be great. I am going to be an archaeologist too, and I am going to play the saxophone, and dive underwater with sharks."

My stomach lurches: I don't mention the 'A' word (asthma), but it crouches behind us, the nightmare ready to intrude into daydreams.

I ask Brendan what his plans are. They haven't changed either: actor, movie director, baker, and swordmaker. He spends a lot of time making storyboards and writing treatments for the movies he is going to direct and star in. Drummer Island and Star Wars 7 are

"ready to be filmed. I just have to write to Steven Spielberg and

*George Lucas. I forgot to send
them an email during the
Christmas holidays, and now I
am just so busy!"*

Swords and sword-making are critical: he needs

"about a thousand"

for Drummer Island. Bren was planning to make The
Hobbit, but Empire magazine (too expensive; he paws
through it at Margiotta's, but doesn't buy it) recently had a
still from Peter Jackson's version, currently in production.

I think about my plans when I was 7: first woman
President of the US, vet, and writer. I am glad no one told
me that grownups usually have to choose one, at most
two, career dreams to chase. Kids need to dream big to
figure out who they are, and the dreams fuel the drive to
get there.

New items on my to-do list: get Bren a subscription to
Empire, and buy Tristan a trowel.

UNSULT OR INSULT?

> *"He did it again. Stuart at After School club said Brendan is not allowed to call anyone that word. But Brendan called me it again."*

Tristan is really gloomy. He is sad, rather than angry, close to tears. Tears are a sign of weakness, as far as Tristan is concerned.

> *"What word, Tristy?"*

I keep forgetting that I am not supposed to call him *'Tristy'* in front of anyone, because it is a baby name. He doesn't shout at me—he really is upset.

> *"Delicious scrubby-bubby! That one! I hate it!"*

> *"Tristan, that is not a real word. Brendan was being silly. He is making you upset on purpose, and it doesn't mean anything, not really."*

> *"Oh! So it's an unsult and not an insult. That's no problem. I'll tell Brendan."*

Smiling, he goes off to gloat.

HUGS ARE BETTER THAN WEDGIES

> *"Tristan, which is more*
> *scarier for you, a hug or a*
> *wedgie?"*

Lots of snickering, Brendan and Tristan have been watching
The Simpsons. It is an education in and of itself, The
Simpsons. *'Wedgies'* is a Bart word for something they are
pretty sure is bad, which, in Brother Zone, makes it
GOOD.

> *"Hmmm. I would definitely have*
> *to vote for wedgies, Brendan,"*

Tristan says, snorting hysterically and falling off my bed.

> *"Well, roll over here and let*
> *me give you a hug. I love*
> *you this morning!"*

Brendan is a touchy-feely guy. Tristan, although less so,
agrees, and my Mom antennae twitch. I listen in.

> *"Eeeew. He is putting his penis on*
> *my leg, Mom! That is SO*
> *disgusting!"*

The needle on the Sniggerometer is buried firmly in the red
zone. Lots of shrieking follows, as Bren tries to escape the
hug.

> *"Brendan wasn't hugging me, he*
> *was wedgying me. My penis just*

popped out because I am
wearing boccies. Maybe I prefer
wedgies, Mom. What is a
wedgie, anyway?"

More hysteria ensues. Brendan is outraged. I separate the now-warring parties. Tristan starts coughing, and reports

"I am totally overlaughing
myself! Whew!"

I respond.

"A wedgie means someone is
pulling your underwear up your
butt by holding onto your elastic
and yanking. You have an erection,
which means your penis is poking
straight out. Wedgies are not
supposed to feel good. Erections
can, but sometimes they just
happen for no particular reason
when you are little."

I wish Martyn was here: I am not squeamish, but I can hardly be said to be an authority on penises.

"OH. Well, I definitely like
hugs better. Talking about
erections is a bit weird, Mom.
Isn't she freaky, Brendan?
Wanna play Transformers, and
not give each other wedgies?"

So much for calm, rational explanations that demystify.

34

ADVERBS ARE AWESOME

> "I like running fastly, Brendan. Am I
> like the girl on Spirit Warriors, whose
> power she got is running fastly?"

> "You aren't that fast, Tristan. Not
> magically fast or anything. Not
> faster than me."

> "I can too run fastly! Except if my
> asthma is badder than usual."

> "Besides, Tristan, 'fastly' is not a
> real word, or even an adverb.
> 'Badder' isn't either. Mrs. Gillies
> has been teaching me about
> adverbs."

> "What is an adverb, Mom? I don't
> want Brendan to tell me. I hate it
> when he bosses me about words!"

> "An adverb is a describing word that
> works on verbs. Verbs are action
> words, words about doing things.
> Adverbs have 'ly' on their ends—that's
> how we can recognize them."

I will hate it if Tristan loses his love of words, and stops
playing with them.

> "'Fastly' has 'ly'. It is MY adverb.
> You can use it if you like, Mom."

*"I think I'll just use 'quickly'
instead, T, because lots of people
know what that means. But thanks
for sharing your word."*

> *"You guys are annoying me! It is
> NOT a real adverb, like 'totally'.
> I am going to always say
> 'quickly'."*

Brendan is 7: a very procedural, do-it-right age.

> *"Brendan talks dorkily, doesn't he,
> Mom? Dorkily, with an 'ly' on the
> end? An ADVERB, Brendan. Did
> you hear it? I hate it when he
> bosses me. I HATE adverbs now."*

*"Enough, guys, enough. Tristy, if
you don't want people to laugh at
you, it might be better to say
'quickly' next time."*

> *"Brendan, could you please quit
> ruining all of my inventioned
> words? Or else I might have to
> crush your skull slowly. Hey! Is
> 'slowly' an adverb? Woo hooooo!
> Adverbs are awesome."*

And so are boys, even when they are inventing things to
fight about, actually.

SNOW CHOCOLATE

> *"Tristan, I think snow tastes*
> *the best when you catch it on*
> *your tongue like this..."*

Brendan demonstrates, and falls up some stairs. Tristan is too busy trying to catch some snow himself to comment on Brendan's spectacular fall. He is also busy thinking.

> *"Brendan, snow tastes really good*
> *all the time unless you scrape it off*
> *the sidewalk, and you get mitten*
> *fuzz or dirt mixed in your snow."*

Tristan doesn't seem finished yet.

> *"Bren, do you think it tastes*
> *better than chocolate?"*

Brendan gives the question the consideration it deserves.

> *"Maybe. It tastes better than*
> *the milk chocolate people give*
> *kids, because they think kids*
> *don't know what is good, and*
> *will eat anything sugary."*

He eats more snow. Tristan eats more snow, and

> *"chillys myself out."*

They agree that Lindor chocolate wrapped in red or black wrappers is waaaaay more tasty than snow, but only if it isn't

> *"too warm and gooshy, 'cause then*
> *it is a bit vomity."*

WIENER-FACE!

> *"He's doing it again."*

Tristan sighs. Even though I'm pretty tuned in, I have no idea what *'he'* (presumably Brendan) is doing, and don't know why Brendan is doing *'it'* again.

> *"What is Brendan doing, T?"*

I bite the bullet.

> *"He keeps telling me that I suck.*
> *Over and over. He does NOT*
> *mean like this."*

Insert your own demonstration here, lips pursed and pooched out.

> *"What do you think he*
> *means, Tristan?"*

Martyn tries not to smile. This is clearly serious stuff.

> *"He means I suck. I am rubbish.*
> *Can you put him in Time Out,*
> *'cause he's just showing off 'cause*
> *his guest is here."*

I am surprised to hear T using the word *'guest'*, but his explanation is plausible; putting your little brother down when your friend is over is *de rigueur*.

*"I won't put him in Time Out,
Tristy; you know you don't suck,
and Brendan is just showing off."*

Martyn is using Patient Dad Voice. Tristan knows that
resisting Patient Dad Voice is useless. Tristan gallops off,
chortling to himself. We laugh when we hear him shout:

*"Brendan! YOU are a
wiener-face!!"*

Remarkable powers of recovery.

MOM IN THE LAND OF THE WEIRDIES

"Tell Mom that again, Brendan!

[snort snicker snort snort]

*You are better at speaking the
language of our ancestors."*

Tristan can barely stand, so great is the burden of hilarity
upon him. I am not in Kansas anymore. I am in Oz,
Brother Zone style. Time and silly things like getting to
school have no meaning for flying monkeys from The
Wizard of Oz.

*"Goolongoo bitey bitey smacky
smacky. HA! Gaweegy mongoosey,
Brendan!"*

*"Mnanga mnagna kwor
kwor, beddeby boolabby
monanga monanga.
Mogga woggy larga
larga."*

Lots of agitated hand waving. Brendan is very serious
about this. I wonder what exactly it means.

*"Spanky wanky penis weenis.
Cacharga! Dorothy! Wonderful
Wizard of Oz! Witchy witchy poo
poo fingle twinkle little–u star–u."*

Tristan is also very serious. I remember reading about the land of the Houyhnhnms. I am playing the part of Gulliver. I wonder if I should try to join in or not.

"*Flargy? Flargy snargy?*"

I am hesitant, questioning: it is not *my* game, and I don't know the rules. Tristan laughs and shouts

"*Gwaga fu hanga*
Liopluridon?"

My comeback:

"*Schooly wooly. Jacket baggy*
boy boys. Spanku bottomy you
no listeninee."

Screams and frantic zipping of jackets follow, and we march out the door on our way to Munchkinland.

INFINITY IS STILL THE WEIRDEST NUMBER OF ALL

"It's really weird. It's like it has a forcefield or something. Other numbers will just bounce off, won't they, Mom?"

"I don't know, Tristan. I know that infinity minus infinity is still infinity."

"Mom, is it a bit magical? I think it is a totally WEIRD number. I remember Tim's story about the hotel with an infinite number of bedrooms. I wouldn't want to have to make all of those beds! I think I might prefer the times tables."

Brendan is oddly practical sometimes. Apart from the magic bit.

THIS BATTLE IS PERFECT

> *"...or at least it will be, if*
> *Tristan ever battles properly. He*
> *keeps defending himself when I*
> *am attacking his Dinosuchus! I*
> *hate it when he cheats!"*

Inward groan. Must… remain… patient. Brendan
is trying to rigidly control what is happening, because he
needs everything to look perfect. He does this when he is
worrying about something he isn't ready to talk about.
We'll just have to put up with Diva Director behavior
until he feels safe enough to talk.

I point out that defending and attacking are normal battle
activities, and in no way constitute cheating. I tell him
that it isn't a movie set, and we aren't filming, but I will
take a picture so he can write the script later. Brendan is
still sulking. He has spent 45 minutes creating a diorama,
while Tristan waited to play. Tristan is officially finished
waiting.

> *"Why do you have to make so*
> *many rules up, Brendan? Why*
> *can't you just play? Why can't you*
> *just act like a normal child?"*

> *"Because I totally want to cool Mom out.*
> *Duh. You need to pay more attention,*
> *Tristan."*

Cool me out? It is Brendan who needs to pay attention;

a mutiny is in process. Tristan is kicking Brendan's army over. And stepping on the fallen, just for emphasis. Brendan threatens to exterminate him. I offer to put everyone in Time Out. I try to explain to both of them what I think is going wrong. Tristan points out that the same things go wrong every time—and he is right.

'Battle' means something different to each of them. Brendan wants a show of force, rank upon rank of minions marching into battle at a civilized hour. Brendan's Britishness shows, at times like these. He believes in queueing, hierarchy, and procedure. Tristan is a guerrilla fighter, a contra, and he is contra everything that smacks of rule or domination. Being contra is one of his principles, as everything looking just right is one of Brendan's.

I can understand both perspectives. I just can't bring the two points of view together—yet. The Momming, the mother-ing, is in the trying.

ANCIENT GEEKS

"I think it is more funnier if we
talk about them like they are
ancient Geeks, Brendan, and not
the Greeks! That's much more
hilarious!"

"Yeah, and Medusa is an old
granny, and Polyphemus can't
eat Odysseus because he's lost all
of his teeth, and he walks with
a stick like this…You do it,
Tristan, I love it when you are
being an old guy!"

"You be an old lady, Brendan.
That's your best one!"

"Do you want to play with our
mythology guys, Tristan, 'cause
we could have a real battle
now, 'cause I don't need to have
a bath tonight, 'cause Dad
didn't tell me I smelled like a
sheep when I got home."

I have to interject at this point.

"On what planet is it OK to
postpone bathing until
another MAN complains

about how smelly you are?
I have seen your father pick a
pair of jeans up off the floor,
smell them, make a face, and
then put them on anyway?"

"What did ancient Greeks
wear, anyway? Do you think
they did the smell test, too?"

"Brendan, I think the Spartans
probably invented the sniff test."

"Cool! Wait until I tell
Mrs. Smith!"

Men are repulsive. And I don't think Mrs. Smith is going
to want to know about smelly Spartans or anyone sniffing
anything. I feel another terse teacher-y note in my future.
Maybe he'll forget by Monday.

King
Zombie

Zombi
miniú

ROBERT EINSTEIN AND BILLY BONKERS' BREAKTHROUGH

> *"WABOOOM! I need some*
> *water. I need some more.*
> *Need some more, need some*
> *more. MOOOOOORE water.*
> *Then, I need to shake it and*
> *mix it up a lot, like this."*

Robert Einstein is nothing if not thorough. His measurements are precise. Billy Bonkers seems… less enthusiastic. Robert tries to persuade him that something important is happening, and it is fun.

> *"We are actually doing real*
> *science, Billy Bonkers. We*
> *really are. I like bathtub*
> *science."*

> *"The thing is, I don't know any*
> *scientists—well, I don't, but I*
> *have NEVER heard of REAL*
> *scientists doing science in the*
> *BATHTUB, Robert Einstein. I*
> *don't think this is real science."*

The sneer is getting louder and bigger.

> *"Billy! Don't SAY that. We*
> *have a science tube here, full*
> *of bubbles and cells and skin*

*bits and maybe some soap. It
is definitely going to turn
into something. I am going to
just dump it in the bucket,
and fill up another one, and
if you close your eyes, you will
get a great surprise."*

*"Whatever. And you just poked
me in the testicles with your
foot, Robert Einstein: Mom
needs to do some nail-cutting
science, thank you very much!
Nope. No one does science in
bathtubs."*

*"Let me just add one single
drop..."*

*"Hold something still,
Robert! I'll hold it now."*

*"What's that again, Billy
Bonkers? What's that called
again?"*

Sigh.

*"A TEST TUBE. Do you
not know ANYTHING,
Einstein?"*

*"Test tube. Test tube. Can I
have the test tube now?"*

*"No. You are the assistant,
remember?"*

"Pour it in. Pour it in. You are too slow, Billy Bonkers!"

"You don't have anything in the bucket yet. You can't transform anything yet."

"Well, I'll put in a crocodile, then. I did it. Pour one tiny drop."

"I'm gonna make it grow two heads. I can't believe I am making it grow two heads, Einstein! This is so exciting!"

"It growed two heads! It definitely growed. I'm gonna turn it back into one. Give me the test tube now. It's my turn. Let it go! You can't drink the chemicals! Let it go! You are growing two heads, professor!"

"Pretend sometimes we're a bit silly, and we drank the chemicals in the lab late at night. Cheers."

"Uuuuum, Professor? I think you are growing two heads again."

"Hello. Bonjour. Hello. Bonjour."

Billy Bonkers giggles, and talks out of one side of his mouth, then the other.

> "My name's Mike, and my name's Einstein."

>> "No it isn't! I'm Einstein. Robert Einstein. And I am changing into a moose from these chemicals.

>> I AM ROBERT EINSTEIN, AND I AM A MOOSE.

>> MOOOOOOOGH!

>> MOOOOOOGH!"

> "Quick! Drink this! You can reverse the procedure, Robert. Drink this, and you won't grow lady boobies."

>> "Brendan, WHY do you always want to talk about boobies? Are you in love?"

> "Tristan, you are changing the subject, and ruining the game. I'm telling! MOM! He isn't being Robert Einstein any more, and he is talking about boobs again!"

I decide that it is time to end the bath, and the game, for today, before it turns as dirty as this bath water.

ROBERT EINSTEIN IS NOT ALONE IN THE BATH

*"I'm still Robert Einstein, but you'll
have to guess who he is,"*

he says, with an exaggerated sigh of patience, pointing at
Brendan. Brendan is absorbed in trying to fill a 2 liter
plastic bottle with their so-called test tube, and announces
that

*"bath science is a little
different today. We've got a
submarine."*

*"But why are you filling the
sub with water? Aren't people
usually worried about
keeping them afloat and
dry?"*

Brendan reacts predictably to my attempt to use logic on
him. He giggles, snorting water all over me, and
announces in his best English accent

*"we want it to sink. That's
the idea. I am filling it up
with our testicle tube."*

Tristan sniggers, and starts shouting

*"that it isn't A TESTICLE TUBE,
Richard. You know you are
Richard the Eighth, and that tube
has your heart in it! How can you
keep talking, Richard, when your
heart is out of your body?"*

Yeah, *'Richard'*, how are you managing that, exactly? Richard informs us that it is definitely a

> *"willy warmer. A testicle*
> *bottle like the Egyptians*
> *had. The reason I died,*
> *Robert Einstein, is that even*
> *someone as great as me can't*
> *wee without his little hoogly*
> *googlies, so I died."*

Robert Einstein sighs again; some people will never learn, clearly.

> *"No. You mean you can't*
> *sperm without them. And*
> *you don't need to do that*
> *right now anyway, Richard,*
> *because you had rubbish*
> *ones and that was why none*
> *of your boy children lived to*
> *be the King."*

Richard is delighted with this more exciting, spermy version of history, and spits water everywhere. He tries the test tube on for size, and finds that

> *"I can fit my wiener in, but*
> *it feels really freaky. No!*
> *Stop that!"*

Robert is angry, and tries to grab the tube.

> *"Give me back my test tube,*
> *Richard, or I am spitting all*
> *over your wiener!"*

Richard quickly complies, but, alas, Robert spits bath water on his wiener anyway, and shouts that he has

"invented the more realer
willy warmer. Spit and bath
water are both super warm.
Dork."

History is a lot weirder than I thought it was, and the scientific method seems to involve a lot of spitting and insults. I should know better than to ask questions; I should just wash their hair in blissful ignorance.

*"Have you got the test
tube, doctor?"*

> *"No! I can't find it! I lost it
> under all of the bubbles. Just a
> minute, Billy Bonkers. Nope.
> Wasn't the test tube. I found the
> Elasmosaurus. Keep looking."*

*"I AM looking, Robert
Einstein—you butthead."*

The boys are playing in the bath with a little plastic tube from the bottom of a flower that has long since died. I ask what the game is.

> *"Robert Einstein and Billy
> Bonkers—obviously."*

Excellent withering scorn, Tristan, really first-rate.

*"I know, Tristan, but what
are Robert Einstein and Billy
Bonkers DOING?"*

> *"Bathtub genetic engineering.
> It is less messy."*

HAIR DON'T

*"Tristan you ask her.
I don't know."*

Brendan almost never admits ignorance. This is going to be complicated.

*"Mom, did Albert Einstein
discover, I mean invent,
hairdos? And I know he isn't
really called Robert—that is
just a pretend game."*

Tristan has asked a question with an easy answer.
I suspect, though, that he quite likes Albert's style.

*"Nope. I can categorically
state that he did not invent
the hairdo. Most grownups
probably think his hair was
messy and weird, and
wouldn't call what he had a
style so much as an accident."*

*"Oh. I think most adults
are nerds. 'Cause you have
to admit, Mom, he had
awesome hair. My other
question is when did he get
dead, anyway?"*

*"I'll ask Martyn to look it
up. I don't know."*

I have been instructed NOT to call Martyn 'Dad', or any other such babyish terms. I report back.

> *"He died in April 1955, and*
> *was born in March 1879. He*
> *was 76 when he died."*

Tristan still looks annoyed. Brendan is

> *"pretty hungry, but I actually*
> *quite like Einstein's hair; let's go*
> *eat breakfast. When your hair is*
> *longer, Tristan, I can help you*
> *stick it up like Einstein's."*

little lighting Bolt

Feathers twings

SWEARING IS DANGEROUS

I am a founding member of the Bad Moms Club. Anyone can join—we aren't an exclusive establishment, with a long and noble pedigree and a constitution. We have no code of conduct. Which is exactly the problem. On Saturday, according to my overly-reliable source, Brendan, I used

"several bad words"

during a (recurring) argument with Martyn (ref. number 207– A, less formally known as what-in-the-world-are-we-going-to do-with-ourselves—and-where-and-when-are-we-moving?). One of these words was *'asshole'*. Tristan, overhearing this, decided that what I had said was *'asshold'*, which probably makes more sense than *'asshole'* when you are 5.

Whatever. The hideously amusing horrible bit was finding out that this is what Tris thought I said because he called Brendan one, mimicking me precisely:

"You are SUCH an asshold,
Brendan. You NEVER listen
to me. Ever."

Ouch.

'Asshold' has now entered the family lexicon, unfortunately. I saw one happening, as we walked up the steps to the flat. Brendan was giggling maniacally as he pinched Tristan's little round butt with both hands. I did my best to look ashamed and suitably downcast, but feel certain I failed, as I have so many other things. The shocked grand dames of Fettes Row will undoubtedly let me know.

THE WEB IS LESS COOL THAN I THOUGHT

"Mom, can you look at something,
I mean, look up something?"

"Yup. What and where?"

"The rarest animal that is the
most endangered. Look it up in
the intergnat, please."

"T, it isn't called 'intergnat,' it is the
'internet'. I know you don't like to get
words wrong, and you don't want Bren
to tease you."

He is a proud creature.

"But MOM! 'World Wide Web?
Web is an arachnid word. 'Gnat' is
an insect word. Spiders make webs
to catch insects!"

"The World Wide Web just means
computers, wires, phone lines, all
connecting to each other."

"Mom, that is a lot more boring
than I thought it was. Pretty much
geeky and nerdish. I liked how it
was in my imagination."

"So did I. Turns out some people are fighting about which is more rare, a tenrec or a tortoise."

> *"When I'm an adult, or maybe a teenager, I think I'll go find out. And then I'll save them from the brink of extinction. Like Nigel Marvin, in Prehistoric Park, only more realish. Do you want to come with me?"*

"Yes. I do. Anywhere."

YELLOW MAKES PEOPLE HAPPY

We are on a stately pilgrimage this morning on our way to
Holiday Club. Slowly, slowly, we rattle and shoogle
through Edinburgh. I HATE having to use the spare tire,
and hate going slowly, and hate even more the thought
that I will be doing 48 mph on the A1. The other Named
Driver, who shall remain nameless, banked my car off a
curb and popped the front left tire.

> *"Mom! This is so AWESOME! I
> hope your car can be like this all
> the time."*

> *"Bren, we'll have a yellow wheel and
> this tiny tire for a day, while the guys
> at the repair shop make sure the real
> wheel and tire are OK."*

I'm not sure he hears me; he is busy waving to everyone we
pass. He is a one man wind-farm.

> *"Mom! Everyone is looking at us!"*

Tristan shouts. He is waving too.

> *"This is the most jazziest your
> Honda Jazz has ever looked. And
> your yellow wheel is SO loud!
> Kinda like ZZZZZZd ZZZZd every
> time we start rolling again. I want
> to keep the yellow wheel too. I
> actually agree with Brendan."*

*"So? Can Tristan and I
paint all the wheels?"*

I wonder if they can agree on a colour. Brendan, predictably:

*"I think dark pink
would be best."*

Nope. Tristan will never acquiesce to pink. The outraged
shriek is almost instantaneous.

*"You can put pink on your
side of the car, stupid. Ugh.
Pink makes me puke in my
brain. Eeeew!"*

I have never been happier that I drive a leased Honda Jazz
cripp-mobile. This is one clash of colors and world views I
don't have to referee.

*"Sorry, guys; it isn't really
our car, so we can't paint
the wheels. Just enjoy the
yellow one."*

They start waving again, because

*"people are still looking,
Mom, 'cause the yellow
makes them happy."*

STANDING IN LINE, SOMETIMES WITH ENEMIES

"Mom, do you like it?"

He is *'doing sideways looking'*, and seems to be in a serious mood. He is also bored. Brendan has been in a line for 35 minutes to use the F1 race car simulator, and the line is bringing out something nastily territorial in all of the adults in the vicinity.

"Tristan, even I need more of
a context than that. I don't
know what your question is
about, so I can't actually
answer it."

"Is 'context' another word
for 'clue'?"

"Yep. It usually is a clue having to
do with time, or a location,
something like that, that lets the
person listening to you zero in on
what exactly you are talking
about."

"I am asking if you like
standing in lines. You do it a
lot. Also, I like that word
'context'. It sounds really, really
special."

"Nope. I don't like waiting in lines
even a tiny bit. But sometimes there
doesn't seem to be any other way of

*getting something done, and a line
forms if LOTS of people need to get
the same thing done."*

> *"Like paying for food, or getting
> money out of a money machine,
> you mean?"*

*"Yep, and I am in line to pay for food
a lot, because you eat a lot, and so does
Brendan. Both of you are growing
really fast, and we always seem to be
running out of milk."*

> *"I still don't like standing in lines.
> Maybe I would like it better if there
> was a TV or a video game console or
> something. But then maybe people
> would never get anything done, and
> lines would take even longer. Why do
> grownups get so angry if they think
> someone is trying to cut in line in
> front of them?"*

*"Why do you get angry if someone
does that to you?"*

> *"I only get angry sometimes, if one of
> my deadliest enemies tries to do it, and
> I am trying to stand behind one of my
> friends. Do grownups just have loads
> of enemies, then?"*

*"I don't know. Some of them
might. How many deadly enemies*

do you have?"

"Just all of the smoochy girls who try to boss me—about 7, I think. And they all want me to say I am going to marry them. I am not going to marry anyone. I am just not in the mood."

TROUBLE WITH THE STEREOPHONICS

We are listening to the Stereophonics' latest CD, Keep Calm and Carry On. It is the one CD that Brendan and Tristan don't fight over; we have a problem with antithetical musical taste. Brendan loves anything with a beat, dance music and R&B; Tristan likes complexity and angst and lots of guitar. Brendan loves Madonna. Tristan suggested that his music school class might want to sing Blur's

> *"Song Two, even though it is the*
> *seventh song on the CD, actually."*

His teachers declined to add Song Two to the lesson plan. I am pleased that they can agree on one CD, even if I am getting a bit tired of it. They had an intense discussion about lyrics this afternoon on the way home from judo. A line in 'Trouble' ends with the phrase, *'...there's no money in this town.'* This is apparently a travesty. Life would not be worth living, etc.

> *"Brendan, this is a totally great*
> *song, but I don't ever want to go*
> *there. I would hate to be somewhere*
> *where there's no money!"*

> *"Yeah, so would I. I love money. It*
> *is one of our favorite things. We*
> *look for it everywhere, don't we*
> *Tristan?"*

> *"Bren, with no money, we couldn't get*
> *candy or Beast Quest books or*
> *computer games. Or even skinnies!"*

*"I guess there's no money in Wales;
that's where the Stereophonics guys
are from. So let's not go there."*

I point out that there is money in Wales—they have
money in their piggy banks that has Welsh symbols on it. I
mention that money is a relatively recent invention, and
for most of history, people traded things to get what they
needed. Farmers made cheese from extra milk, for
example, and gave some of it to a man who fixed the roof
of their barn. They feel sorry for the putative farmer,
because he probably didn't have any Beast Quest books.

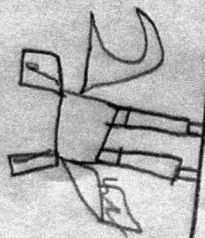

DRAWING PICTURES IS DANGEROUS

*'I am not sure if you'll be
able to manage it, Tristan,
but I think you might be
able to draw a thrilled
lizard."*

Brendan has strong views about what babies like. Preferably
something gentle, or, at worst, boring and educational. He
has already forbidden ninjas (menacing), blue ringed octopi
(poisonous), and the Grim Reaper (scary)—all of which are
Tristan specialties.

*"A thrilled lizard, Brendan?? Why
are you trying to make me draw a
HAPPY lizard?" Tristan still wants
to make a rhino or a cobra.
Brendan is trying to tame him,
and he doesn't like it. He is also
baffled; when has a lizard ever
needed a smile? Surely my
stepsister, whom he has never met,
won't expect reptiles to have facial
expressions, like something out of a
Disney cartoon?"*

*"Thrilled, Tristan. A
thrilled lizard,"*

Brendan says, aiming for ironic, bemused detachment. He
rolls his eyes at me.

*"He is only five and a
half, Mom: do you think
he is too young to draw
a thrilled lizard? Should
I do one?"*

I suggest that the word Brendan may be looking for is
'frilled', meaning ruffly and lacy-looking. Brendan agrees. I
explain that thrilled with a *'f'* sound is frilled, and with a
'th' sound means happy. Comprehension sort of dawns.

*"Oh, OK, that sounds
complicated, so I guess
I'd better draw it."*

Tristan announces that he is drawing a rhino. Or perhaps a
dragon. Maybe something poisonous,

*"because the world doesn't only
have cuddly things in it, Brendan,
and the baby will need to know
about other stuff. She might even
be interested in science, Brendan,
unlike YOU."*

Good use of withering scorn, Tristan. I will award you two
points, which Brendan will never credit to your account,
because his world is a magical realism one, in which a
frilled lizard is likely to also be thrilled.

INVINCIBILITY CAN DEFEAT BOXER SHORTS

*"My penis is being really
invincible, Mom! It keeps
poking up!"*

*"T, I don't have one, so you'll need
to explain your problem a bit
more."*

*"No, it is just being
invincible and not bendy,
and it keeps poking down
and out the leg-hole of my
boxers."*

We've discussed this before. Boxers are cooler-looking, but
have certain... drawbacks, like *'bunching'* (which has
already happened twice today, if reports are accurate), and
'squashing', when boy bits don't stay where they are
supposed to stay. I offer a Grandma Helenism that has
never made any sense to me:

"Pride has no pair."

Tristan responds with a snort and wanders off to ask
Martyn what to do with a recalcitrant penis. I hope Martyn
knows what recalcitrant means, or Tristan will be back.

BROCCOLI AND BRAVERY

> *"Mom, what does 'valiant'*
> *mean?"*

I have never made it this far into a day before being asked
what something means. Tristan is full of questions about
words. Must have been a slow day, words-wise: guess
there's not much call for thinking once you've voted, and
come home to play computer games all afternoon until it
is time to get ice cream.

> *"It means brave, and courageous,*
> *and people usually use it when they*
> *are talking about someone who keeps*
> *trying to do something even when it*
> *seems like it is going to be impossible.*
> *It isn't a word we use about someone*
> *who isn't afraid, but about someone*
> *who tries their best."*

> *"So does it count as valiant*
> *if I eat this broccoli with*
> *my eyes open?"*

> *"Knowing how much you hate*
> *broccoli, I would have to say yes, if*
> *you keep your eyes open and keep the*
> *whining and fake vomiting to a*
> *minimum."*

"I like it that you know lots of words, Mom, because I am curious, and I love words, but I wish you didn't know quite so much about vegetables."

"I love you too, Tristan, and I wish you would be a bit more valiant about your vegetables. Now get busy!"

"Mom, what if I never like broccoli? What if I never like brussels sprouts? Will you still love me and think I am valiant?"

"Yes. Yes, I will, even if you never like them, ever."

He chews determinedly, exaggeratedly, with his eyes open, and grabs his milk and takes a big chug to wash down the offending greenery. I congratulate him on facing his fear of broccoli.

MARTYN THE GIANT KILLER

Martyn became a heroic figure at 8:17 a.m., BST, 8/5/10.
He managed to emerge unscathed from a duel with a

"totally much huger,
terrifying creature"

[Clark, Brendan. 8:15 a.m. BST 8/5/10, personal high-
pitched and high-volume communication] The creature
was sighted at 7:57 a.m. by T. Clark, who reported it to the
Maid (me) immediately:

"It is zooming around the
living room, and stopping on
things, and making an angry
noise like this

ZZZZZZZZZZZZ!!

TTTTTTZZZZZZZ!!

every time it crashes into the
window. I think it's gonna
break a window pane, Mom, so
can you get out of bed and
come because it is really pretty
massive, and also I think I
might need a snack, which
means I need to be in the
kitchen and not in the living
room, although this is my
favorite show after 'Deadly 60'.
But I'm not scared, though."

*"Dad will chase it out. The
wasp just came in because it
was so cold last night. The wasp
doesn't want to sting you or
Brendan. He just wants to get
out, and the window confuses
him because he can see out but
not get out. I am getting in the
shower."*

My reconnaissance mission over, I asked the Wasp Inspector
(Martyn) to come to the living room. Your correspondent got
out of the shower at 8:19 a.m. BST. I didn't hear any blood-
curdling screams. The TV was still on. Martyn appeared to be
in exactly the same spot in bed (e.g., WAY too far over into
my side). The boys were putting on their judo gi. I asked
Tristan where the wasp was.

*"Dad took care of it. I don't
think 'wasp' is a scary enough
name; something like 'wasc'
would be better, cause that
sounds more deadlier, like 'orc'.
Dad is so awesome. He is the
best Dad ever. I can't believe how
he did that!"*

*"What did Dad do,
Tristan?"*

*"I don't know. The 'wasc' was
just suddenly GONE."*

The Wasp Inspector confirmed that he had opened the top
window, and the *'wasc'* had gone *'right out'*. Heroism and
wry understatement like that are what make Britain great.

> *"Why is 'Dad Time' different from REAL*
> *time, from time on the clock? But 'Mom*
> *Time' is always exactly like the clock,*
> *especially when I don't want it to be, and I*
> *want your minutes to be longer? And can*
> *Dad not even tell the time properly? He must*
> *be the biggest dork alive!"*

Brendan is annoyed. He is waiting for a chance to play games on the computer, and he has been told *'in 15 minutes'* 4 times. Brendan is right: Martyn's conception of time is not often linked to time the way we measure it and keep it, but to time the way Martyn feels it. I can sympathize. This used to drive me crazy, and make me feel undervalued: I felt that if Martyn wanted to see me, he would be on time. Now I always triple Martyn's estimates of how long something will take, and am pleasantly surprised if he is finished sooner.

I talk to Brendan about the fact that time often seems to slow down when you are waiting for something fun, and goes really fast if you are worrying about something or don't want something to happen. I also mention that he can look and see that Martyn is still working on the computer. This is my evidence, though, and Brendan is only interested in his evidence, in the fact that the clock says 15 minutes have elapsed some time ago.

> *"'Kid Time' is accurate; it doesn't change*
> *except if I am doing homework, and then*
> *it slows waaaaaaay down."*

I give up.

SOME CHUPACABRAS ARE WILDER THAN OTHERS

A chupacabra, or *'goat sucker'* (trans. from Spanish), in case
you are wondering, is a vampiric animal that looks a bit
like a dead, bloated, hairless coyote that has been baking at
the side of the road for several days in either Mexico or
Texas, take your pick. The legend of the chupacabra seems
to have merged with sightings of aliens; some chupacabras
are apparently bipedal now. Call me cynical. I grew up
hearing and seeing coyotes, and they are just not very
menacing. Smelly when dead, or when eating dead things,
yes, but not scary. ANYWAY.

Brendan is obsessed with chupacabras, but his
interpretation of the legend is pretty tame; smiling, almost
toothless, zombies don't scare anyone. Tristan's is much
grimmer, in keeping with his little black heart and psyche.
Chupacabras are

> *"fast, stealthy, almost normal*
> *looking, but really ugly, and you*
> *can only see them out of the corner*
> *of your eye and then WHAM! They*
> *bite you."*

What follows is a transcript of a local chupacabra sighting.

[Tristan, holding 3 plastic swords]

> *"Chupacabra!!! I came to Mexico to*
> *spy on you! And I saw you sucking*
> *blood from a goat. You looked like*
> *you enjoyed it, you fiend!"*

[Brendan]

> *"Giggle. Snort. Snort. Yes! I*
> *love blood! It tastes like*
> *strawberries and butterflies!"*

I wondered at this point if perhaps Brendan's version of
the legend was a bit poofy.

[Tristan, using *'angry eyes'* and *'thunder eyebrows'*, to try to
get the chupacabra to BEHAVE]

> *"You like blood and meat*
> *soup. You drink goat's blood.*
> *You love goat's blood: you tear*
> *the heads off of goats, and hold*
> *them in the air, and let the*
> *blood drip down! But you don't*
> *love goat blood as much as*
> *GIRL blood!*
>
> *Moowahwhwhahaha!"*

[Brendan, smiling still, and waltzing across the bedroom,
sure of his audience's attention]

> *"Chupacabra want bite*
> *you! Are you girl? Please be*
> *girl! Girls taste like berries*
> *to chupacabra!"*

[Tristan]

> *"Brendan! Chupacabras are*
> *VAMPIRES.*

*They don't need to ask anyone's
permission to do ANYTHING!*

*Play it the RIGHT way or I AM
LEAVING, you BUTTHEAD!"*

[Brendan, giggling victoriously, because he doesn't want to
be the chupacabra]

*"Pooga ooooga
Gwal gwak!"*

Swords. Shrieking. Snorting. Parents attacked. Mayhem.
Turns out the small blond one with swords IS the chupacabra.

EVERYONE SHOULD HAVE A PET BRENDAN

I wonder if he was a dog in a former life. He is loving, smells slightly lanolin-ish when his hair is wet, enjoys leaning against the radiator, just being cozy, routinely stands on my feet, likes to be in constant physical contact with everyone in his environment, and drools a bit (especially when drumming). Brendan getting his head or back scratched slides into an ecstatic trance. He will eat whatever is put down in front of him, even if it is only an hour since he had a huge breakfast. He likes licking bowls and pans. And he loves, loves, loves, riding with his head and a paw or two out the car window, tasting the air as it goes past. I think everyone should have one around the house; this one, however, is not for sale. He is ours.

ENJOYMENT OR DESTROYMENT?

> *"I'm NOT thinking about enjoyment, Brendan. When I eat sour cream cookies, I am thinking about something different."*

Brendan looks up, icing on his chin, crumbs spilling out of his mouth,

> *"Ut oo finkin' abow?"*

> *"I..."*

said Tristan,

> *"...am thinking about DESTROYMENT. Destroyment of all of the cookies. That's what I'm thinking about. Destroyment is like enjoyment, only more better."*

Brendan looks at the plate, counting.

> *"You can't do destroyment to all the cookies; it won't be fair, and my enjoyment will disappear."*

> *"Stop talking, Brendan. I am doing destroyment. My ears are shutting, just like my eyes."*

HADES IS THE AWESOMEST

"Do you really think so?
I think it is Zeus."

Brendan is hierarchical in his tastes, and pretty traditional. My vote would be for Poseidon.

"Yes. I seriously do think so.
Hades has lots of power, and
people stay with him forever.
They don't mostly get to escape
like Percy Jackson did. And
Hades tortures and scares
people. Sometimes, Brendan,
'awesome' doesn't mean good. It
means super bad and terrible."

"Yeah, but sometimes super
terrible is powerful, Tristan,
just like you said. Do you
believe in the Afterlife? Do you
think you are just dead, and
that's it, or do you think
something else happens?"

"Hmmm. I think there is an
Afterlife. I don't know what it is
like. Sometimes people maybe get
changed to ghosts or shades, like it
says in our mythology book."

*"Tristan, why do we keep talking
about death and blood and guts?
Do you think it is because we are
boys? Girls don't talk about war
and that sort of stuff, at least
Mom doesn't."*

Brendan isn't sure this is a good thing, all this talk of
'Death and War and Hell'.

*"I think we talk about blood and
death because we think they are
awesome. Not the good kind."*

Tristan is pretty sure about this. And sure that it is important:

*"because if we don't think about
it, then we might just be scared.
And maybe you are gonna be a
dog or something if you come
back to life, Brendan."*

*"I think I'll be a Great
Dane. I haven't decided
what color."*

Brendan relaxes. That's an Afterlife he can support.

I PREFER NOT TO CALL THEM CRISPS

"*I just don't like doing it.*"

"*Don't like doing what,
Tristan?*"

"*Saying 'crisps'. It just doesn't
sound right to my ears. And it
feels weird to me.*"

"*Why does it feel weird?
Where I am from, people don't
call them 'crisps,' so it feels
strange to me if I call them
'crisps'.*"

"*It just sounds weird. Like there
are two 'S's guarding the 'P'.
And 'S' is not a crunchy-
sounding letter. And why does
'P' need guards?*"

I wonder why, too. What does '*P*' have to be scared of? Would
something bad happen if it just stood there, naked,
defenseless, on the packet?

90

THE WORLD CUP ACCORDING TO BRENDAN

> *"You don't understand.*
> *You just can't."*

[gusty, heartbroken sighs]

> *"I was occasionally*
> *thwarted during my*
> *own childhood."*

Actually, my childhood was mainly about being thwarted, but he doesn't need to know that to get the sarcastic undertones.

> *"I didn't always get*
> *what I wanted, when I*
> *wanted it, yet I*
> *survived."*

The eyerolls and angry stomping suggest Brendan is not convinced that I can know the pain of being 7. He does not believe that I, Mom, did not emerge, adult-sized, from a pod on some alien ship, shortly before being beamed down to Earth to take on the role of Evil Overlord in the spellbinding drama that is His Life.

> *'I can just tell you don't*
> *understand. And what is*
> *even more terribler is that*
> *you don't care. You don't care*
> *about my feelings at all."*

[lips quivering, voice trembling, Brendan exits stage left]

I do remember what it is like to be deprived of allowance.
I remember what it feels like to not have the same clothes,
shoes, toys as everyone else. He is right, though: I have
never known the pain, the exquisite agony, of being unable
to buy Match Attax cards at Tesco (and thanks, Tesco, for
putting the cards in all of the bags of apples from South
Africa—way to ruin the scheduled life lesson). Sunday
afternoon on the eve of the World Cup, when

> *"everyone in my class has*
> *them. I kind of like*
> *them now,"*

is apparently a great day on which to buy Match Attax.
Brendan is not really interested in football/soccer. He does
like sharp uniforms, however, and has picked Argentina to
win. He would have picked Everton, but they can't play in
the World Cup

> *"for some weird reason,*
> *like rules or something."*

Match Attax cards are a good way to look like you care
about Scotland's true religion, The Beautiful Game. I
won't deprive him long.

SHOW AND TELL IS RUBBISH

> *'Everyone liked my 'Show & Tell',*
> *only they didn't really believe it was*
> *me playing drums on the CD, so my*
> *teacher played it again and I showed*
> *them how it looked. Then they knew*
> *it was me.'"*

Hmmm. Not necessarily a good thing. I have visions of Bren
in the old days. I had to surreptitiously mop the drum kit,
because there was a direct relationship between the amount of
drool he produced and the difficulty of using two sticks and a
foot pedal.

> *"But the thing is, he ALWAYS*
> *has a rubbish Show & Tell."*

Brendan is referring to his frenemy, a boy who manages to
be cool and creepy, friendly and abusive, all at the same
time. I tell Brendan that no one could have a worse *'Show &*
Tell' experience than I did; my mother made me bring my
little sister, so she could be rid of her for the morning. I am
still emotionally scarred, 35 years later. Brendan agrees that
this was a terrible thing, and wonders how Grandma Helen
could do

> *"anything so evil, when she is*
> *always smiling in pictures."*

He tries to explain.

> *"His Show & Tell is always*
> *the same——awful. It is just*

random stuff he finds on the
way to school. Nothing
unusual."

"Like dead bugs
and stuff?"

I know the frenemy. I know what he likes.

"Yeah. Once he brought some
trash in from the playground.
He tried to say it was an
antique bottle, but it was
plastic, and I couldn't see a
genie in there."

I can understand this might be a bit disappointing. I ask what today's contribution was.

"A piece of wood he said
looked like an ear."

Brendan is scathing. I ask if it looked like an ear, even a tiny bit?

"Nope. But my teacher said it
looked a lot like an ear, 'cause
she felt sorry for him, but she
had to look down at the floor
behind her desk for a minute. I
think she was laughing."

I do too. I was.

STARING YOUR DAD DOWN DOESN'T ALWAYS WORK

Brendan and Martyn decided to have a Staring Contest. Both of them believe they are Staring Contest Champions. Brendan practices

> *"quite a lot at*
> *school... I beat people*
> *all the time."*

Martyn's staring prowess was apparently legendary in high school.

The problem was that they both got bored. And their eyes started to dry out. Which is never a good thing. Optimists, each thought they could turn the boredom of the other to their advantage. They accidentally had a Blinking Contest instead. The Blinking Contest (Brendan won, by the way; sorry Martyn) was much more fun to watch, as far as Tristan and I were concerned:

> *"Mom, they look like they*
> *have brain diseases!"*

BREAD WOLVES ARE A BIT LIKE SHARKS

They are sniffing under the door as I climb the stairs. I hear them whispering. And, possibly, slobbering, though that may just be the toothless 7 year old one. They are wondering if I went to Valvona & Crolla, the little snobs. Nope. Just Waitrose. I was getting their progenitor a roast chicken; I didn't want to make two stops, OK? They squabble excitedly, and talk about me in the third person:

> *"What do you think she is*
> *bringing us for lunch,*
> *Brendan?"*

And

> *"I don't know—but I hope*
> *she isn't going to make us*
> *try artichoke hearts again!"*

Don't worry, beastly offspring; I didn't get any. I think Martyn still has some olives left.

'She' is unloading groceries first. Eventually, table set, the Bread Wolves approach cautiously and begin nibbling their prey. They look around for vegetables, and are relieved to see carrots. The wolves seem generally approving, and wag their chunks of bread at each other while crumbs fall out of their mouths onto the carpet.

Looks like 'she' will have to vacuum after lunch, when the wolves have slunk back to their den and their father has sloped off to nap.

THE BEST FOOD ON EARTH

> *"...is OBVIOUSLY salmon."*

Tristan doesn't want any discussion about this.

> *"Salmon is the most best*
> *because it is tasty. It tastes the*
> *best with salt and pepper, the*
> *way Grandpa who is also*
> *your Dad likes to eat it.*
> *Dinner is perfect when I*
> *have salmon or fish fingers.*
> *Or else fish and chips.*
> *Especially if other people*
> *come to eat the fish and chips*
> *with us at our house."*

It is now clear to me: the best dinner things are fish and company.

> *"Ice cream after dinner is also*
> *perfect, Mom, so can we have*
> *that, too?"*

Yes, we aim to please at the Clark Restaurant.

GHOSTLY SEAWEED AND DEAD CRABS

We tried to look for fossils at the beach (Joppa) today, and got distracted. Not many fossils in evidence, maybe because the tide was coming back in, and most of the jagged sandwiches of Carboniferous coal and sandstone and shale, turned sideways by earthquake faults and volcanic activity long ago, were under water. We saw white seaweed, other kids, dead crabs, worm poop, live crabs, and bladderwort. We stomped the bladderwort (recommended) and smelled the dead crabs (not recommended) and made them wave to each other (surprisingly satisfying) until they disintegrated. Brendan found a love heart, which almost made up for the obsessionally scientific way in which Tristan made him watch while he

> *"stroked the anemones until*
> *they shut—that is SO cool,*
> *isn't it Brendan?"*

We need more fossils, though; a bit of coal and a shard of long-ago tree fern bark have only served to galvanize us.

SUPER BIG BLUE EYES

Tristan asked why people like babies so much. He is torn: he loves them and then very abruptly really wants

> *"to be away from them, like in a different universe or something, where I can't smell their poop or hear them screaming."*

I know what he means. I told him that our brains are programmed to make us want to take care of babies, in part because babies look helpless and cute. I asked him if he wanted to know a weird but true fact about babies and eyeballs. He, being Tristan, did. Our eyes don't grow much, I said. When we are babies, our eyes are as big as they are ever going to be; they change shape as we get bigger, but stay pretty much the same size. People like creatures with big eyes, like baby humans and animals.

> *"But not like Cyclops big or anything, cause that would be seriously freaky,"*

he responded, before deciding to

> *"bigger my eyes so I can always be the littlest."*

I like Tristan's eyes even when they are slightly too biggered.

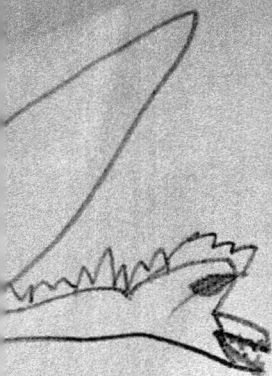

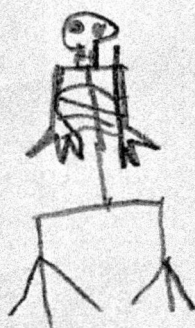

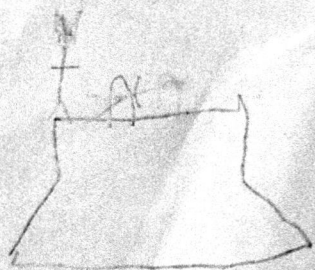

DOING MANLY THINGS WITH DAD

The Male Bonding Father's Day Trip was a resounding success. Apart from getting sand in their jersey boxer shorts, Tristan would like for me to add. Brendan rattled off an extremely LOOOOOOOONG list when I asked them what they had done, after I collected them from the beach in Dunbar.

> *"Well, first we almost nearly missed the train. It left at 12:50. And we didn't get to eat at Burger King because we only had 8 minutes, and we had to get sandwiches for lunch at the Co-op, AND there was only one train between Dunbar and Edinburgh on Sunday, because it didn't turn around and it kept going."*

Martyn mentioned that they were on the Inter City superfast train to Plymouth, and people around them were torn between irritation at their enjoyment of being on the train and amusement. The boys apparently narrated everything. Tristan thought the best thing about the train was

> *"that it goes WOAH and then WHEEEEEE when it went on a curve, and made me tip over a bit. That was SO cool."*

Brendan's list continued:

> *"We saw lots of peoples' houses. Tristy got brave enough to talk to a lady. He told her we weren't*

*on holiday, or rather I did, when
it was me who was doing the
talking. She was friendly. When
we got to Dunbar, we had to ask
people where the beach was.
Some guys near a leisure centre
told us. Then I chose a cozy place
to eat on the rocks. We used our
pink picnic blanket. Then we
spent ages by the rock pools, and
we saw 3 green crabs and some
hermit crabs and some real, alive
shrimps that scooted backwards,
which were a bit scary."*

Tristan objected:

*"They were not SCARY, Brendan,
they were just like armoured
arthropods. I didn't find a single
fossil, but the shrimps scooched away
from my fingers and Dad's".*

*"As I was saying, MOM. We saw
some hermit crabs too, and I
wanted one for a pet. We saw
some unusually tiny brown fish.
We climbed on rocks and into a
cave with an eyeball painted on
the back wall that looked like
mysterious Egyptian
hieroglyphics."*

*"Brendan, I thought only I
knew that word. I am
impressed with you."*

Tristan is complimentary.

> *"I liked that cave as well. I would
> like to go there every day."*

> *"Ah-HEM. I am STILL telling
> her, Tristan. We also NEARLY
> fired a cannon, but we didn't
> have any matches and I think
> the cannonballs were missing or
> else glued down."*

> *"Don't forget to tell her about
> nearly interrupting the bowls
> game, and every one of the old
> people getting fussy."*

Martyn was perhaps a bit tired of being with the boys by this
point.

> *"We caught a jellyfish,
> and it died."*

I raised an eyebrow at Martyn.

> *"It may have been a little
> bit dead already, but it is
> possible that we may have
> hurried it along slightly."*

Martyn and Tristan considered the possibility that they
may have loved the jellyfish to death. After a moment of
silence in memoriam, or maybe a short nap, Tristan
changed the topic to sand eels:

> *"We actually caught one,
> Mom, we didn't just see it!*

And Brendan touched it! And they were just like Ron said."

"NEXT..."

said Brendan acidly,

"...we talked to some nice grannies. They were from Northern Ireland, and they were on holiday. I still don't know why Dad thinks that is where they were from, because they certainly didn't tell me."

Martyn and I tried to tell Brendan that it was possible to know where they were from on the basis of their accents. Brendan still seemed dubious, and changed the subject.

"And that was all we did, except for walking about 100 miles, the different beach, seeing the weird tubey sorts of worms that make a sand cocoon around their bodies, walking some more, getting soaked by the waves, Tristan getting really cold with his teeth chattering because you took too long to find us...and that's all, really. Except maybe you should come on the adventure next time, because you remember things like extra clothes, or maybe you could just pack a back pack for us and stay at home until we need you. OOOH. My butt feels much better in this warm car."

I took them home, where they had a *'triple shower'* and ate lots of meat and other manly food before crawling into bed. The boys are saving their ticket stubs from the train, and Martyn is saving a beautiful rock from the beach.

DRUMMING IS GETTING LESS PAINFUL

Brendan can maintain a rhythm now, much to our relief (and, I am sure, our neighbours'). Tristan is not calling it *'Dumbing Practice'* any more, and is jealous, which Brendan likes.

> *"Tristan isn't the only one who*
> *is good at something in our*
> *house, is he? I am pretty good at*
> *drumming. Maybe even*
> *excellent at it. Maybe*
> *drumming is my special thing,*
> *like running and being clever*
> *and being cute are Tristan's."*

I wish Brendan knew how cute and clever and special he was —I guess being big and clumsy and a bit drooly when you play the drums isn't exactly confidence-building. Tristan is planning to take up the electric guitar as soon as

> *"someone buys me one for*
> *Christmas, 'cause Santa isn't real,*
> *and, plus, he probably isn't into*
> *rock and roll."*

Brendan, meanwhile, is contented to keep drumming, and drumming, and drumming a little bit more after that, because drumming is something he can do, something that is his.

ALL HAIL THE UNHOLY ROMAN EMPEROR

Today the boys are having a shower. They want to watch a few minutes of the Spain v Portugal World Cup game, and showers are (usually) faster than baths. I soap them up, throw the washcloths over the shower door, and rush off to start the dishes, shouting instructions about scrubbing between toes and rinsing hair.

It quickly becomes apparent that they have seen far more of Monty Python's Life of Brian than is perhaps strictly necessary (Martyn?).

> *"I am the Unholy*
> *Roman Emperor!"*

Brendan shouts. Tristan responds with

> *"And I, your majesty, am*
> *Biggus Dickus. Are you*
> *waughing at my name? What*
> *is so funny, my fwend?"*

They chant *'Biggus Dickus'* seventy or eighty times while throwing water at each other and fighting over the small showerhead.

I remind them that they wanted to watch some football, and need to hurry. Tristan wants to know if I think

> *"Biggus Dickus is a totawy*
> *hiwawious name."*

After a moment's thought, I concede that it is better than Teenius Weenius. I have once again been defeated by the power of testosterone and man humor: if you can't beat them, might as well (temporarily) join them, in the hopes of steering the conversation into more palatable channels. I suspect it won't work.

GROSS SPURT

"Why do grownups always say that? Everyone says it about Brendan, and I think it is insulting. It means getting more worser, doesn't it?"

"What means getting worse, Tristan?"

"Gross spurt. It sounds really nasty. Monstrous. Monsterous. Like boogers or puke or something. Gross spurt. Yuk. It even sounds wet."

"It isn't 'gross spurt,' T, it is 'growth spurt'. Grownups say that to kids when they seem like they are getting bigger every day, or when they suddenly need a new coat or new shoes."

"I thought it was because Brendan is so dirty and sticky all the time."

"Nope. Nothing to do with how sticky Brendan is. I agree that he gets pretty dirty, and he

leaves handprints on things all the time. I don't know how he manages it."

"I know. He's always licking his fingers instead of using water, or soap, or a towel. He sometimes just dries his hands on the towel after. I tell him it isn't the same. He says he likes to be 'unhygienic'—but what does that even mean? Is that the same as 'disgusting'?"

"More or less. I'll talk to him."

DISCARDED CLOTHES

I pick up the pile, and it is still warm. These clothes were shucked by Brendan about 20 minutes ago, and never quite made it into the laundry basket. School uniform, socks, underwear; all seem too big to belong to you, but not too dirty. You've been busy: spaghetti sauce, milk, pen, pencil, mango smoothie, other stuff I'll never be able to guess. I'll put your clothes straight into the washer, then go in to check to make sure your covers are pulled up and you haven't fallen out of bed—yet. You are so big and so little, Brendan, and I love you. But your socks reek, and I think I'm gonna leave them for you to pick up.

SPIDERS ARE STILL BUGGING US

"Mom, I think I am going to
be alive longer than you."

"Yep. Probably. I am a lot older
than you are, and I am likely to
die before you do. Are you worrying
about dying again?"

"Nah. Not really. Well, possibly a
tiny bit. But I think I will be alive
after you get dead, and I'll think
about you a lot."

"Well, I don't really know what
happens when people die. Maybe
I'll be in heaven. Maybe I won't.
So how are we going to know who
really lived the longest? Will we see
each other in heaven, and you can
say 'Hah! I'm the oldest now, 'cause
I lived to be 93' or something like
that?"

"Yeah. That would be good to do.
Unless we get recycled."

"You think we'll be
reincarnated as bugs or
something?"

"I know what bug I would

111

*want to be. I want to be a
mosquito and suck blood like a
vampire. What would you
want to be? I'll bet Dad and
Brendan will say 'butterfly.'"*

*"I think I want to be a
Goliath beetle, one of those
really big black and white
ones. But being a dragonfly
sounds pretty tempting."*

*"I'll ask them and tell you
what they say. I'll be back
in a minute!"*

Five minutes pass. Martyn and Brendan are talking, and
Tristan has to wait (oh! the agony!) to ask his question.

*"Mom! They didn't say
'butterfly.' Dad is planning
to be a praying mantis and
Brendan wants to be a
Goliath Bird-Eating Spider!
That's the most ungirliest
thing he has said in ages!"*

PLAYING AT FIGHTING

"You are gonna gret this!"

Five Year Old Fists of Fury(TM) are flying through the air, attached to a maniacally-grinning body. Tristan is all muscle and bone. Whatever *'this'* is, it will definitely hurt.

"What am I gonna regret?"

Martyn tries to do a bit of language modelling rather than correcting Tristan overtly. Brendan is around, and if he picks up on Tristan's error or overt correction, there is likely to be blood and further violence.

"You are gonna GRET this. Watch out!"

Tristan pointedly, definitely means *'gret'*. Brendan has now chimed in, offering to make Martyn

"gret that I'm here too."

Martyn may officially be in trouble, yet he appears to be looking forward to *'this'*.

"What am I going to regret, you brats? Hrm? You still haven't told me!"

Martyn tries again, and fails again, as far as Tristan is concerned.

> *"I haven't did it to you yet. You are only going to re-GRET it when I do it to you again, over and over and over, like this: punch punch punch tackle punch!"*

He springs, like the predator he is, into the air, with a blood-curdling shriek.

DRUMMER BOY

Brendan sprinted up the stairs to our flat, judo gi flapping like a cape. He wanted to do drum practice

> *"as soon as possible."*

Not a bad thing: getting to go straight from doing your

> *"second most favorite thing"*

to

> *"your best thing."*

Brendan

> *"totally needed"*

to get the drums set up the right way,

> *"just like Taylor*
> *Hawkins' set up."*

Martyn found the Complete Drum Nerds website, and they looked at diagrams. Brendan noticed that he was 3 cymbals short of a full Hawkins. He has bravely coped with the disappointment, helped along by discovering that he has the same brand of cymbals (Zildjian). Brendan thinks Taylor is

> *"nearly as good at drumming*
> *as John Bonham, and way*
> *better at staying alive."*

Tristan is planning to get the same guitar as Jimi Hendrix,

> *"but not kill myself with*
> *drugs and needles."*

Hmmmm. Must find them some less… exciting role models. It may be too late.

LUCKY CHARMS

His spoon bounced off the faucet, and fell into the sink.
Brendan announced that he was lucky because

> *"I'm wearing my lucky*
> *charms. I take them with*
> *me everywhere."*

Sniggering commences.

> *"What is a lucky charm, anyway?"*

Tristan is a bit skeptical.

> *"I don't believe in luckiness.*
> *Where are your charms,*
> *Brendan? Show me them."*

Hands on hips, working the *'thunder eyebrows'*, he looks very
stern.

> *"My nipples!"*

Brendan shrieks.

> *"My nipples are my*
> *lucky charms, just like*
> *Fantastic Mr. Fox's tail*
> *is his lucky thing!"*

Tristan has another question. More of an excuse, really, than
a genuine question.

> *"Where is your lucky charm,*
> *Dad? Mine is right here*
> *between my legs. That's my*
> *lucky charm."*

He smirks. More Y-chromosome hilarity. Ugh. Far too early.
Not enough caffeine. Brendan tells Tristan that

> *"Mom doesn't have a lucky*
> *charm. That's why she can't*
> *control Dad."*

Hysterical hooting from Martyn. Tristan, bristling, rushes to
my defense:

> *"Don't be so stupid. Mom's*
> *lucky charms are her*
> *boobies."*

Both boys lift up their shirts, as if on cue, and I feel
compelled to refuse their kind offers to show me their

> *"lower lucky charms*
> *as well."*

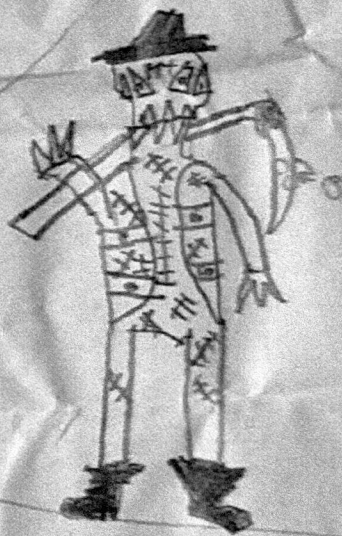

PRIMARY 2 IS HARDER THAN I THOUGHT

"Why do you think it is so
hard, Tristan? Was today not a
good day?"

He is a festering boil of '5 and ¾' year old grumpiness.

"I told you already! It was
RUBBISH."

"I know that's how you
feel. I want to know why
you feel like it was
rubbishy."

"It just was. I tripped a lot. My
trousers are too long. Or maybe it
is my new shoes that are the
problem. I was clumsy, and I'm
usually never. And I hardly never
even got to play. And actually, I
miss P1. I miss my old teacher. She
always noticed if I used 'wow'
words. Today I just got to write 4
words! My time was totally
wasted."

"It was just the first day. You
probably need to wear a belt,
and that would keep you from
tripping over the hems of your
trousers. You are definitely not

*a clumsy guy. I think your new
teachers will figure out that you
can do more work, and you'll
get to write more, and they will
notice that you know lots of
'wow' words. What is your
favorite 'wow' word at the
moment, anyway?"*

        *"Nothin'. I don't know any good
words like 'excruciating'! Does
that mean the same as sore,
'cause if it does, then I do still
know about 'wow' words, and
I'm still clever."*

*"It does. Your brain is working just
fine, Mr. T., and tomorrow is
'wearing your own clothes to school'
day, so you won't trip over your
trousers."*

        *"Are my skinny jeans with the
leather patches clean? 'Cause if I
wear them, and wear my AC/DC
T-shirt, I'll feel more normaler."*

"That can be arranged."

Small things make small people feel a lot better.

PLURALS

Tristan wanted to know why *'bra'* was singular, when

> *"there's obviously TWO boobs to be concerned about. If you have two boobs, you should be wearing two bras, because 'bra' and 'boobs' both end in plural 's'. I'm learning about this stuff, Mom, because I'm in Primary 2, so don't feel bad if you don't remember it 'cause you are really old."*

SNOGGING

> *"What is 'snogging', Mom?"*

Manic giggling from both boys. I am trying to get them to finish breakfast, so we can leave for school. It is definitely Monday. Both are unrepentant and non-compliant, as we health professionals love to say.

> *"You know what 'snogging' is,*
> *Bren. You don't need to ask me.*
> *Why are we talking about*
> *snogging, anyway?"*

> > *"It is teenager kissing, Brendan,*
> > *and I know you want to do it*
> > *with someone. I know you do! It*
> > *is lots of spit and tongues going*
> > *like this"*

[WARNING: revolting demo involving cereal]

Tristan's tongue is zooming in and out of his mouth like a chameleon's, carrying an ever-decreasing load of Frosted Shredded Wheat with each pass. The table is covered in a fine mist of spit and fiber. Brendan, giggling and blushing, attempts to defend his own honor.

> > *"It isn't me. Someone told me*
> > *that someone else wants to do*
> > *snogging to ME, Tristan. And*
> > *you can guess who it is!!"*

*"Oh, yeah, I can for sure guess
that, Bren, 'cause I know you want
to lick down her throat!"*

*"Ok, ok, that's enough talking
about snogging for one morning.
We've got to get to school. Tristan,
you need to consider the
possibility that Brendan may not
really be in the mood to snog
anyone. He is 8; he may just
want to hold her hand, and kiss
her on the cheek."*

*"Mom, do you like snogging Dad?
Do you and Dad still roll around
on the floor putting your tongues
together? That is just so disgusting.
Bren, you pretend to be Dad, and
I'll be Mom:*

*'Oh, Martyn, please lick my lips
like I'm a big ice cream.'"*

I threaten to snog both of them at school in front of everyone
if we are late, and they shriek off to brush their teeth.

THAT'S MY BOY

As I hobbled out of the school gates this morning, someone I'd never met before stopped me. She asked me if I was Brendan's mother. I said yes, I was, and asked if she had a child in his class. It is generally a safe thing to be asked; all people usually want to say is that Brendan is '*Enormous—is he really only 8?*' or '*Very gentle*', or '*He has been followed out of Tesco / the library / the doctor's surgery by my toddler, and could I please retrieve him/her?*'

Being asked if I am Tristan's mother is a little more stressful—I could be asked anything from '*Is he only 5?*' (yes), to '*Does he really have an electric guitar?*' (also yes), or '*Why does my son call him 'master'?*' (you really, really don't want to know—he might be creating zombies), to '*How on Earth does he know so many big words?*' (I use them, he listens), to '*Does he really worship Damon Albarn, and practice a religion called Albarnism?*' (Not… exactly, and do I look like some sort of liberal freak of a parent who would let their son listen to devil music? I do? Shit). What I'm trying to say is that it is generally fine being asked if I am Bren's Mom. Brendan's only sin, in the eyes of other parents, is playing the drums, and even that can be blamed on my nefarious influence or Martyn's.

Today, I found out that Brendan organized lunch for his friend X after X got a nasty cut in the lunch scrum. X came back, bandaged, thinking everything good was gone. X had the last baked potato. I was really touched that X's Mom had made the effort to talk to me. Most people don't really notice Bren; he leads and influences quietly.

I thanked her for telling me, because I hadn't heard anything about it.

When I asked Bren about the incident, he sounded a little embarrassed. It turns out that he had been delighted to give X his baked potato, not that he wasn't trying to take care of X. He got

> *"meatballs instead. It was so GREAT that I gave away my baked potato, Mom! I wasn't sure there was going to be anything good left, but I wanted X to not be sad."*

Brendan is a happy-go-lucky human being; he expects good things to happen to him, and they generally do. May his bread always land buttered side up, and his plate of meatballs be full.

ONE LAST TIME

Tristan is sad. He doesn't

> *"feel ready for winter yet, and the
> leaves are starting to change."*

He wants

> *"one last trip to the beach
> before I have to put my shorts
> away."*

He doesn't like the

> *"in-between months—August
> and September are boring, with
> no good holidays."*

I ask which month is a good one. He rolls his eyes.

> *"A—hem. October! Duh! My
> birthday, Halloween, new
> winter coats, darkness!"*

So today is a day of one last summer things. Skipping stones
at the beach, jumping from rock to slippery rock, wearing
shorts even though it is cold, finding dead crabs. Important
things. And, because we are very lucky, a small green, irascible
live crab with

> *"lots of beige brothers that are
> too little to catch without
> crushing them, so I'm just
> watching them and keeping
> them safe."*

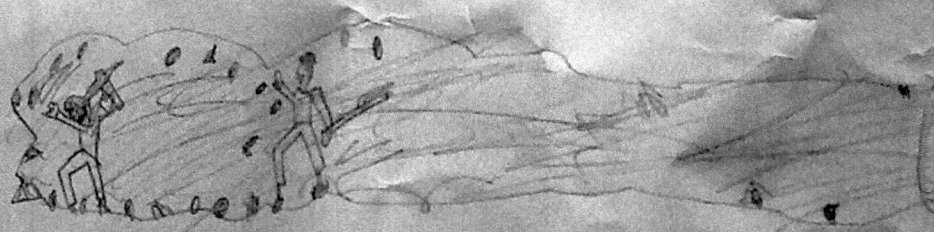

Tristan's *'thunder eyebrows'* are almost a mustache. He is glowering like he has never glowered in his life before. The focus of his ire? His new reading book. As far as Tristan is concerned, the developers of the Oxford Reading Tree scheme need to burn:

> *"does anyone EVER make grownups read this rubbish? I think the writer and the drawer need to go to Hades forever."*

He spent the first two weeks of the summer holidays reading as many non-educational, age-inappropriate things like Beast Quest, and as much Greek mythology, as he could get his hands on. He loathes Biff, and Chip, and Kipper, and keeps hoping that the Magic Key

> *"will get changed into a nuclear weapon and they will all get turned to vaporized skeletons. Now THAT I would want to read about."*

I sympathize. I didn't do the reading scheme thing, not because the nuns took pity on me, but because they were keen to keep me quiet. They let me read whatever I wanted. I don't want him to lose his love of reading, and I don't want any more raging, screaming battles to get him to finish reading 12 short @%&*ing pages so that I can tick the box in his homework diary. So Martyn has come up with a plan. Involving BAD words. I will suggest that Tristan gets to call them Shit, Crap, and Wiener whenever he does his homework. I hate to think what he's gonna call Fluffy.

WHAT DOES THAT EVEN MEAN?

"Mom. I have a question."

"Not a surprise, Tristan.
What is the question?"

"How do you spell Ms.? And what does
that even mean? My new Head
Teacher is a Mizz. She said that that
was her name, not Miss or Mrs."

"I would spell it with 'Ms,'
but I would say it so it sounds
like 'Mizz,' just like you do.
Some people prefer to have
that as a title, rather than
Mrs., just as some people
prefer to keep their maiden
names. What do you think it
means?"

"I think it means she doesn't want
anyone to be able to guess straight
away if she is married or not, 'cause
that isn't their business anyway. It's a
bit like a secret code."

BRENDAN THE BRAVE

Brendan is still a footie (soccer) virgin. Practice was cancelled today because the rain was so heavy. He has his first game as a goalie tomorrow, and he and all of the other boys have studs (spikes). I am not amused. I don't see why eight year olds need spikes.

Brendan tends goal sternly, stoically, with his face. He comes home from school scarred by contact with the pavement from diving to save goals. He plays badly and with absolute commitment. He pays attention (mostly). He belongs, and he loves it. I hope he still loves it after tomorrow morning.

> *"Who made words up in the first place, and gave them their name?"*

If in doubt, or coffee has not kicked in yet, stall for time, and get more information.

> *"What name?"*

> *"The name WORDS, Mom. Who gave them THAT? Why do we use WORDS, anyway, and how come I was borned not knowing what all of the WORDS in the world are, and what they mean? It is really FRUSTRATING being a little kid sometimes!"*

Tristan is not a patient person, especially with himself. Hmm. Where to start, exactly? Can't dumb down much, and still have what I say be accurate, not with these guys. I dive in:

> *"I don't know who first called words 'words'. The Bible says that in the beginning there was the Word, and the Word was God. Lots of people think humans started using words thousands of years ago, maybe more than a hundred thousand years ago. Some people think we had a proto-language, a sort of mini-language, like chimps or gorillas or ground squirrels have, for a long time before we had 'proper' language. We started writing things down thousands of years ago."*

Deep breath, check to see if they are still with me—they are. The 60 second Intro to Linguistic Theory continues.

> *"Words don't get called 'words' in every language: in French the word for words is 'mots' and in Spanish it is 'palabras'. Everyone is born not knowing all of the words; something in our brains starts soaking up words and how to make them, probably even before we are born, from the talking that we hear all around us. Somebody called Noam Chomsky named it the 'black box'."*

> *"So our brains are good at making and choosing words from hearing them and remembering them? That's OK, then. I guess I can catch up when I get bigger. I still wonder why there are so many of them, and why they are so mysterious. I can't always guess what they mean. Why do we need them, anyway?"*

> *"Tristan, can you please ask thingy to give you the thingy that thingy asked you to thingy?"*

> *"Huh? Are you crazy, MOM?"*

> *"If we didn't have lots of different words, for all of the different things we see and hear and smell, how could we tell anyone about them? Some people I see in the hospital*

*have had strokes. Their brains have
trouble making and understanding
language and words. They get really
frustrated and sad and exhausted
trying to tell everyone how they are
feeling, or what they want for lunch.
We need lots of words, is the answer."*

*'Are they like the lady we saw at the
Botanics, Mom, who had a
wheelchair, and just cried and said
'hello' a lot, and holded your hand, no
matter what anyone else was saying?'*

"*Yes, Brendan, exactly like that.*"

*"Tristan is right. Words are mysterious.
I'm glad my black box isn't broken.
That would be terrible. And I'll bet
you can't get a new one, and fit it into
your brain, can you? Because people
are squishier than computers. They
would get damaged."*

"*Mmmhmm. People parts are not
so easy to replace. That's why we try
to take good care of our brains.*"

I love talking to them about words, about language: they
share my obsession, Tristan especially so, with language in all
of its beauty and ugliness, in all of its capacity to nurture and
to hurt. I wonder when the name Noam Chomksy is going to
be co-opted for a game or a show. It might be an unsult, an
insult, a title, an adverb: Brendan and Tristan like using their
black boxes.

*"You are SO a melodrammer,
Brendan. You do melodrama all
the time and you make a
ginormous fuss about not getting
your own way, and sometimes you
cry when you watch sad movies
and stuff. And you do melodrama
very way much more than me."*

*"Melodrammer is not a word, is it,
Mom? And I am not as much of a
one as Henry is, even if it is an
actual word. I don't think it is."*

*"Melodrammer is not a word, as
far as I know, but I don't think
there is a special word for someone
who is very melodramatic, other
than BUTTHEAD."*

*"Hahahaha, Mom. VERY funny.
Tristan, she is weird, isn't she?"*

*"I still say you are a
melodrammer."*

WORDS ARE MYSTERIOUSER THAN EVER

"I have been wondering about words again, Mom. How come you know a lot of words? And how come Dad knows a lot of different words than the words you know?"

"Dad and I studied different things, and so we read a lot of different things, and talked to different people. Dad doesn't use most of the words he used when he was at university any more, because they are science words, and Dad doesn't think of himself as a scientist any more. But he still likes cool stuff, and some science stuff is cool."

"Well, I like science words, and so do you. Even Brendan does, a little bit. I don't like the word 'tsunami' though, because that sounds scary, a bit like 'werewolf' sounds scary. And that is the mysteriouser part: how can words give us feelings?"

"You are right. We do like science words, especially reptile-y ones. And we like books, and we look at a lot of books. Some words do sound scary, sometimes, I think, if we don't

understand them, and sometimes
because we have scary feelings, and
then we find words to describe the
feelings, and THEN those words
sound scary to us."

> *"I quite like 'werewolf'; I*
> *don't like 'gelatine'. It sounds*
> *disgusting."*

Brendan is right; it kinda does, especially if you say it with a sneer.

I can hear Tristan's dirty belly laugh from just outside the front door of the flat, as I come up the stairs. He and Brendan are clearly discussing something not intended for parental ears. Lots of whispering. Lots of banging. Someone is pulling books off the bookshelf and flicking through pages at high speed.

> *"Here it, Brendan! The boobies painting!"*

More giggling.

'Boobies' is a good clue. This is either the Salvador Dali book or one of their mythology books. I listen a bit more— no mention of melting clocks, so must be mythology.

> *"That shell she's riding on is really funny. And there are smaller ones here and here and here. Do you think her seashell bikini is hurting her nipples, Tristan?"*

Tristan is giggling and snorting:

> *"Yeah, Brendan, but I don't care, 'cause she's a dorky lady. I would be worried… hahahahahah… hooo… haahhahahahha… if it were PENIS the God of Love, 'cause that shell would be sore."*

I'll leave them to it, and tell them about Apollo and Cupid another day.

WORDS ARE SUPER-MYSTERIOUS

"Dad, I still don't understand
why we have words. Or who
invented words."

"Bren, I think we all invent words
all the time. People invent words
together and use them together."

"But who used them first? Who
came up with the idea?"

He's not budging. I hope Martyn isn't feeling complacent. I decide to help out by offering a real-life example. Sometimes Brendan responds to these.

"Remember the other day when
Tristan called you a melodrammer?
That word was his invention."

"Yeah! I remember that."

Brendan doesn't look happy, though.

"And who invented writing? Who had that
idea first? And do you have to be able to
write first before you can talk or after?"

"Who do you think it
was, Brendan?"

Can this be Martyn? I feel a bit odd. Martyn is suddenly sounding like the Voice Of Reason. Either that or my brain is being pickled by the high dose macrodantin.

"It was cavemen. And they wrote on

*rocks. You can write on rocks and with
rocks, right? They used rocks in caves.
You can carve on rocks."*

Brendan relaxes. He has a theory. I am glad Tristan isn't
listening, or he would want hard data. When and where
did this happen? Were these proto-language users Homo
Sapiens Neandertalensis? Was radiocarbon dating involved
in the discovery of these putative rocks? This isn't really
what has Brendan interested. Martyn knows this.

*"Yeah, but that doesn't mean they had
writing. I still think they walked
around going like this*

[demonstrates knuckle dragging]

'ooh ooh aaah aah ugg uuggg.'"

Bren joins in, grunting

"OOOOH OOOOH AAAAH AAHHH

WAAAA WAAHHH UGGG."

He finishes off with a guttural plethora of glottal stops:

"Awh—i' Awh—i' Awh—i'?"

Awh—i entered his vocabulary when our friend Robert
was telling the boys about working in Glasgow, and
meeting someone who said '*Awh—i?*' to him every day,
which, translated from Glaswegian, equates to 'Is that it,
sir?'

Martyn and Brendan decide to invent their own language
tonight. I believe it will be called Brendanish. I am now
setting places at the table for Dinner in the Tower of
Babel. I wonder if Noam Chomsky will join us?

BRENDANISH

Martyn has cracked, at least temporarily, Brother Zone, and is now an *ex officio* member. Dinner in Babel is a roaring success. And I do mean roaring (and hooting, and sniggering, and slamming the table, and spraying crumbs and bits of burger everywhere, and farting). A success limited only by the fact that the menfolks are too busy playing to eat. The first proto-word designated in the new language was actually a sign. A rather predictable first sign: one for penis. I'll let you imagine that one. It was pretty... transparent.

It was followed quickly by the word *'NUT'*, which means meat, *'NUT NUT'*, which means 'give me food NOW', and lots of sniggering and snorting. Peace deteriorated into threats and territoriality. After about 15 minutes of threatening to *'NUT NUT'* everyone's penis, they have decided women must have invented language.

RITUALS ARE FISHY

Tristan has a friend called Big Yellow: a fish who lives in the glasshouses at the Royal Botanical Gardens of Edinburgh. Tristan wants to believe that

> *"Big Yellow knows it's me, and that's why he always comes over, but I think he really wants more food."*

He loves Big Yellow, and I love that he loves Big Yellow. Neither of us is exactly a hard-core romantic, so this shared quirk of ours is special. Brendan began demanding to go to

> *"Fishy Flower Place"*

when he was two. He waddled around contentedly looking and smelling, and I waddled behind him, with Tristan sloshing around his own aquarium inside me. Now, the boys fight over whose turn it is to push the automatic door opener buttons (several are apparently broken: coincidence?). We slink into the Fish Dungeon to see the Bloated and Terrifying Albino Frog. Sometimes he even moves. There is a note by the tank that says he isn't dead; we like that too. Next, we check to see if the daffodils are coming up yet (yup); we look for moorhen chicks (no yellow-toed black fuzzballs yet); we run across the slimy bridge in the rock garden, because this time, there might be a troll there, plus the sign says 'no running'. Pah.

Waste of a good slippery death-defying moment. We listen for the whistle and 'Closing Time' shouts of the staff, and are always a bit sad to hear them. It is part of the magic of the Botanics to be bored, bored witless, thinking about going there again, but we are seduced every time.

JOKER EYEBROWS

"I know you aren't really mad,
Dad. You are doing it again."

"Doing what again, Tristan?
Can't you see I'm looking at you
like I am really, really, angry?!?"

Tristan still isn't buying the whole 'anger' scene. Martyn is trying hard not to laugh, with the result that he looks like he is trying not to sneeze and/or fart.

"You are doing your joker
eyebrows, Dad. When you do
joker eyebrows, I know I'm not
really in trouble."

"I love you Tristan, I
really do."

"I know that Dad, 'cause you
are not doing pretending
eyebrows."

How many looks can one pair of eyebrows have?

Amoeba

Eyeball
Monster

5 horns
1 giant eye!
body with

10
pupils

2 legs
2 ears

ANOTHER VEGETABLE OFF MY LIST

*"Brendan, what shape do
cucumbers remind you of?"*

Snort, snort, smirk.
Snigger, wiggle, insane giggling:

*"Cucumbers should be called...
POOPUMBERS!!"*

Thanks, guys. I used to love salad.

GLOVE MONSTER

"Hey! Look at me, Mom! My hands are on backwards! I look broken and freaky!"

Tristan is waiting for Brendan's drumming lesson to be over. Music School isn't so exciting when you are finished with your own class. In desperation, Tristan has been blowing Martyr's gloves up like balloons, as he has nothing else to play with. The broken hands game and some cuddling rounds out the 50 minutes of waiting nicely.

ARM WRESTLING TITAN

Brendan announced this morning that he won an arm-wrestling match at school last week.

> "I didn't even use all of my
> might; I just did like this with
> my arm, and even with a half or
> just a quarter of my might, that
> was enough."

Tristan and I nodded, and kept eating. Martyn crooked an eyebrow, and used Sarcastic Dad Voice.

> "What did you just
> say? Did you just say
> might?"

> "Mmmhmm."

Brendan is chewing now, and for the first time in his life, is not opening his mouth with food in it.

> "Might? Might?"

Martyn is not dropping this.

> "What do you
> mean by might?"

Brendan sighs.

> "I mean my might. My
> power, my strongness.
> Might."

The 'duh' is implied.

"But might is not the word
people usually use to talk
about being strong. Do you
think you are a superhero or
a god or something?"

I tell Martyn that yes, that's exactly what Brendan is trying to say. *'Might'* has been gleaned from mythology. Most of the movie scripts Brendan writes are about ninjas or gods who like to battle and play the drums. Brendan says, again:

"I was arm wrestling him, and
I just held my arm like this,
and I didn't even have to use a
quarter or a half of my might,
and I beat him. I am like an
arm-wrestling titan. A bit like
the earthquake one in
Hercules."

He puts more cereal in his mouth, chews for a bit, and repeats

"Might. That's why I was
the winner."

He wipes his mouth, and flicks the crumbs from his hand onto the floor.

THE BUSINESS OF CHILDHOOD

"But didn't you have fun
helping me, Tristan?"

Martyn is trying to convince both of us that the time he spent putting in new light switches was exactly what Tristan wanted from Dad & Tristan Time.

"He loves tools and carrying
screwdrivers and wires and
talking about that kind of
stuff."

I try to frame both sides of this non-argument. I know what each of them means. They don't have as much time together as Martyn had with Brendan before Tristan was born.

"I know he does. But that isn't all
he loves, and wasn't quite what he
had in mind. That was working.
Tristan was hoping that he would
be playing with you."

"Dad, the whole thing about life
is to play. Playing is my job.
Playing is always a kid's job.
Holding tools and walking
around talking about electricity
is good, but it isn't the best thing.
The best thing is being with you
and being silly. You are a bit like
a big child anyway."

Tristan is so eloquent that it is hard to remember that he is 5, and that his business is, indeed, playing. Preferably with Dad.

HOMEWORK

> "WHY did anyone ever invent
> homework? Did someone do it
> just to torture children?"

Tristan is a bit tired of his current reading book. Lame stories.
Biff and Chip and Kipper are NOT our fave peeps. Wilf and
Wilma and Floppy are OK, and Gran is ace (she kicks some
witchy butt). On the whole, though, we prefer the Marvel
Comics small graphic novels; we've learned many cooler
words in those. I decide to tell him how it really is:

> "Nope. It was invented to torture
> parents. Homework is a teacher's
> way of getting even with me after
> having to answer your questions
> all day."

> "Really?"

Brendan is indignant.

> "Why didn't you tell me this
> when I was reading the Biff
> and Chip books?"

> "Nope. Not really: homework was invented
> so you didn't have to stay in school until you
> are 35. Unless you want to, of course. The
> idea behind homework is that you practice
> some of what you've been learning."

> "I still think it is torture. You can't
> change my mind."

I wouldn't dream of it.

COLD KISSES

"Brendan, can you see it?
Can you see the writing Jack
Frost left?"

"Tristan, you don't really
believe in Jack Frost, do you?
I think that's from the taxi
turning around."

Brendan isn't usually so unromantic.

"Of course not. I'm 5 now. I
don't believe in any silly stuff.
But I like the way the street
looks. The taxi made an 'X'.
X means 'kiss' in girl language."

"So maybe I should give
you both a kiss, while no
one is looking."

Tristan and Brendan pucker up, eyes closed. I kiss them
before Tristan decides to tell me that 'X' doesn't mean kissing
in Mom language. I stop to take a picture of the three point
turn on the way back from school, before the watery sun hits
the cobbles and my license to love melts away.

I STILL HATE HOMEWORK

"I mean it. I really do."

Tristan eyes me murderously, pencil held in a death grip.
I hope he points that at the paper soon, or I may get
concerned.

*"T, you have to write the word
ending 'igh' 9 times. That won't
take you very long, especially if
you concentrate and stop sulking."*

*"It isn't about how LONG it takes,
Mom; I just don't think Mrs.
Hagart likes me very much."*

*"Tristan, she does. She really does.
She wants you to get better at writing
so you can keep doing cool stuff. She
is sad, and so am I, because you are
so hard on yourself when your
writing is messy. That's why we ask
you to practice a little bit every day."*

*"Well. If it keeps you women from
crying, I'll do it. I still think I
should be working on my computer
mouse skills. That is importanter."*

He is working what his brother calls *'thunder eyebrows'*, so I
try really hard not to laugh. I turn around and pretend to
look for an eraser in the drawer.

TENDERIZED

We are walking and rhyming in the Botanics. Brendan is doing slapstick; Tristan is creating rhyming doggerel to go with Bren's visuals. Brendan decides to try to turn a flip, and ends up whimpering in pain, clutching himself, after inadvertently straddling the top of a bench. Tristan's response?

> *"Oh my dear Brenders, you've
> smashed up your tenders!"*

They both fell to the ground laughing, Brendan still clutching his *'tenders'*.

Men. Honestly.

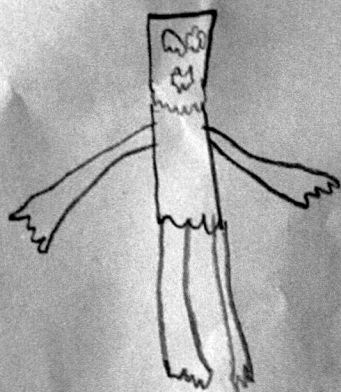

ALIEN SLIME IN BROTHER ZONE

> *"Don't put your slimy*
> *testicles on me again,*
> *Brendan!"*

I am tired. I didn't sleep well. The sniggering is unbelievably loud. The boys are firmly in Brother Zone, and were when I picked them up from holiday club. I somehow have… to… find… the… strength to cook dinner and get them into the bath and off to bed. OK—OK—you know I am not going to bother with the bath. But what does this testicle thing mean? Should I muster the energy for some sort of maternal intervention?

> *"Tristan, keep your*
> *golden shower of*
> *murgatroglacittor away*
> *from my spergnik. I am*
> *an alien!"*

Whew. Good to know. That explains why they are slimy. I'll sit back down.

IT DOESN'T MATTER IF THE RACE IS PRETEND

It also doesn't matter if the people racing you are pretend either. Your brother can still decide that you've lost. Today's fun: a fratricidal moment about a non-race. Brendan asked Tristan if he wanted to race. Tristan didn't want to, because he was wearing his wellies,

"and they are slippery grippers."

Wellies are *de rigueur* on judo days, aka Wednesdays, for three reasons: 1) the boys inevitably step in dog poop in Leith on the way to judo; 2) they then have an excuse to go in puddles; and 3) they are likely to win the race onto the judo mat if they can shuck off their wellies fast enough.

Brendan called Tristan a

"slowpoke baby chicken,"

and pranced off,

"racing two imaginary guys…
and I am beating both of them
by miles. Steam is coming from
my toes I am so FAST, Tristan!"

Tristan:

"I can see them, and you are way
behind. I am catching you and
doing this."

'*This*' entailed whipping him with a judo belt, and looked pretty sore. I don't like being the referee of last resort when some of the contestants are imaginary, and at least two are damn rude.

SUPERMOM VS. THE SNIPERS OF DEATH

They aren't quiet, or far away, or very well equipped. It is
obvious, though, that they are snipers. I know I am being
stalked. I don't turn around. The snickering and farting get
louder.

'General?'

hisses the bigger one.

> *'How can we sort this problem
> out? What would you suggest,
> sir? Should I shoot and shoot and
> keep shooting, until they are both
> dead? What are your orders?"*

The mighty small one responds in a guttural Glaswegian,
rolling his 'r's mercilessly:

> *"First we have to load the
> bullets. Then aim, soldier."*

I casually mention that I've turned my forcefield on. Martyn
nods absently, and keeps reading. He trusts me to defend the
Parental Bed by any means necessary.

> *"Mom has a forcefield.
> What do you think we
> should do, soldier?"*

Herr General has sharp ears. The galumphing First
(technically Only) Lieutenant replies:

> *'Retreat, and plan better, sir!!"*

They commando crawl back to base, aka Tristan's bed, and cover themselves with blankets. Tristan grouses:

> *"thinking always makes you fart, Brendan. I don't want to be under the Blue Fuzzy with you any more."*

Mom 1: Snipers 0

A good beginning, but I won't rest on my laurels. The day is young.

NAPKINS: WHAT ARE THEY FOR, EXACTLY?

> *"There's olive oil all over your*
> *face, Brendan, and crumbs are*
> *sticking in it."*

Tristan looks a bit repulsed.

> *"I know. That's just what*
> *happens when I am eating*
> *crusty bread, and I don't*
> *want to get crumbs or oil on*
> *my hands. I tear the bread*
> *with my teeth, like this, but I*
> *am missing a lot across the*
> *front and it gets a bit messy."*

Brendan doesn't feel that there's much he could be doing differently, in contrast to his fellow diners.

> *"There must be something he*
> *could do, Mom, even though*
> *he doesn't have enough teeth*
> *to keep his food in."*

> *"There is. He could use*
> *something called a*
> *napkin."*

Martyn has noticed that I am getting a napkin out.

> *"Yep. Here's a napkin,*
> *Bren."*

I pass them out; we can all use one.

"You can do something
like this with it,"

I tell him, holding him in a headlock, rubbing it all over
his mouth. He is giggling maniacally.

"What is this weird device? Do
they have these in museums?"

Brendan snorts several oil-soaked crumbs onto the table.
He is incorrigibly messy, and incorrigibly lovely. I will be
glad when he gets some teeth, though.

*"Or I might have to hurt you.
Don't make me angry!*

If I lose my temper... argh!

You did it again!

*Don't... zzzzt... make... zzzzt...
zzzt... me... zzzzzzzt... lose...
zzzzzzzzzzzzzzt... my...
zzzzzzzzzzzzt... temper!*

I warned you!"

Hysterical giggling. Brendan and Tristan are playing Lego
Star Wars. I can't quite figure out who is being whom.

"I am the Naughty Emperor!

ZZZZZZZZZZZT!

*Feel the force of my Dark Side,
Brendan!*

ZZZZZZZZZZZT!"

*"Tristan, I am so glad you really
don't have blue electrocution
powers in real life! You would do
that to me all the time!"*

163

"That's what I am imagining, Brendan!

ZZZZZZZZT!

ZZZZZZT!

I am the Naughty Emperor!"

"I don't like being the Naughty Emperor. He is WAY too ugly!"

"I'll get you for that!

ZZZZZZT!

I am the Naughty Emperor!

ZZZZT ZZZZZT!"

> *"You heard me. I said*
> *'Easierestly'. Four men can get*
> *killed easierestly in Warlord."*

Tristan is adverbifying a lot these days. He runs everywhere *'fastly'*. I ask him why he sticks *'ly'* on the end of everything.

> *"I put 'ly' into things that are*
> *importanter for people to listen*
> *to. 'ly' helps Brendan to notice*
> *that I am talking. But the*
> *problem is, then he tells me*
> *what I've said isn't really a*
> *word. I think it is a word in*
> *Tristanish."*

I think *'easierestly'* is definitely a word in Tristanish. And I think anything that gets Brendan's attention is probably a good invention; he notices modifiers. Tristanish isn't something for public consumption; it is a home language, made in the moment. Tristan knows that he needs to code-switch, and that makes me happy and sad at the same time.

"My taste buds are tired of
fancy food. Can we have
macaroni and cheese?"

Brendan is tired.

"My taste buds are shouting
'that's a great idea!', but they
have tiny voices because they are
almost microscopic."

Tristan has voted in favor of leaving roast chicken with chorizo until tomorrow.

The chicken will be fine until tomorrow. Pasta might be a problem—I will have to use the ends of three different packets. This will require dumping 3 lots of pasta into the water, 2 minutes apart.

Tristan is excited when he sees the final result; 3 different kinds of pasta is apparently really special.

"You have to do different numbers
of puffs to cool off each one. Tell me
all of their names again."

"Fusilli is the curly one;
farfalle is the butterfly-
shaped one..."

"Farfalle looks like mustaches,
NOT butterflies."

Tristan is emphatic. I stand corrected.

> *"Fine. The name means
> butterflies. The half-moon
> shaped one is actually called
> macaroni."*

An experiment is soon underway. Lots of huffing later,
results are announced.

> *"Mom: you need 1 puff for
> farfalle; 4 puffs for fusilli; and
> 6 puffs for macaroni."*

Tristan has confidence in his data.

> *"I think they each need four
> puffs, Tristan. Maybe that's
> because I am a stronger
> breather."*

Brendan has a death wish, evidently. Tristan is out of his
chair, fork first, working his *'thunder eyebrows'*. I tell them
both that the pasta is cooling off, and it is hard for
scientists to all measure things in exactly the same way.

FIRST ONE TASTES THE BEST

We are sitting in the Filmhouse, waiting for Ponyo to start.

As always, Martyn and the boys are in the process of finishing their treats (in this case, Fruit Hearts) before the main feature starts. Tristan announces that

> *"the first one out of the*
> *packet always tastes the*
> *best."*

Martyn and Brendan agree, after immediately conducting some rigorous N=1 testing themselves. I tell Brendan that the concept is called *'diminishing marginal returns'*. He tells me that he is very glad the movie is starting

> *"any second, because that*
> *returns stuff sounds really*
> *boring and I am not*
> *interested."*

I am glad that I don't actually care about diminishing marginal returns, or I would be seriously pissed off. Glad Ponyo is starting. The jellyfish are fantastic.

> *"Tristan, what's your*
> *favorite shape?"*

Brendan is having a geometry moment. He is doodling, staring dreamily out the window, fantasizing about being an architect.

> *"Brendan, I can't believe you are*
> *asking me that. You have a lot of*
> *nerve. I told you a million times,*
> *my favorite shape is*
> *RECTANGLE."*

> *"Tristan, I just can't believe it!*
> *We have the same favorite*
> *shape! Isn't that AMAZING?"*

What I can't believe is how much they sound like polite, well-bred ladies, middle aged school teachers both. Tristan sounds as upset as if Brendan has just asked him if he gets his support undergarments from Marks & Spencer. Is this the start of the slippery slope? Will they sound like Morningside ladies if we live here much longer?

BABIES ARE A BIT FREAKY

They are small. They are red, especially when pooping.
They cry a lot. They are obsessed with eating. Tristan
decided today that he would

> *"rather be a human*
> *than a baby."*

Martyn snidely asked if Tristan thought babies were aliens;
Brendan sniggered and said

> *'Yeah, that's exactly*
> *what he thinks!"*

Brendan is a baby magnet; he loves them and attracts
them, and it is hard for me to get out of Tesco without
having acquired one if Brendan is with me. I once fished
someone who did not belong to me out of our basket and
returned him, screaming in protest, to his mother.

I think I may know what Tristan means, though; babies
are pretty lucky that we're hard-wired to take care of them,
because they are a hell of a lot of work. And I say that as
someone who loves kids. But I will be un-maternal and
admit that I would have preferred them to have cooked a
bit longer (three months?), so that they were a bit more,
well, human and interactive.

Tristan is just not sure what he thinks about babies, or
how he feels about them. Wednesday, he demanded an
explanation as to why I have not had a baby yet, when he
asked,

> *"three days ago, and*
> *THAT is AGES to wait…*

…for ANYTHING."

This morning he asked me to

> *"promise you will never have*
> *one, because then I couldn't*
> *be the littlest any more."*

I don't want to tell him this, but what my grandmother told me is probably true: our children are always our babies, even when we are 70 and they are 40. We had a macho sort of hug instead, and I let him win.

BLOATING IS *NOT* THE SAME AS GLOATING

> *"Stop gloating, Brendan. You*
> *are making Tristan feel bad.*
> *Stop gloating, I said!"*

Martyn is trying to put out a forest fire before it starts.
Brendan is just better at computer games than Tristan is;
the fine-motor coordination issues have had 2 years longer
to sort themselves.

> *"I wasn't bloating, Dad. I was*
> *definitely NOT 'bloating'. I was*
> *just mentioning that I won that*
> *game already, and completed the*
> *level, and it was really easy."*

I would agree with him; he was doing nothing that resembles
bloating. I know a lot about bloating. It involves feeling really
shit about myself, NOT making other people feel like shit.
Bren was, however, gloating, in his infuriating *'I-am-7-and-*
you-are-just-totally-5' way, and Tristan would have hit
him already, but he is holding Martyn's iPhone.

Martyn tries again.

> *"You were GLOATING. Guh. Guh.*
> *GLOATING. It means making someone else*
> *feel small. You didn't need to tell him how*
> *to do the game, and issue orders, and then*
> *make fun of him when he makes mistakes.*
> *You know what? Just go to Time Out."*

Brendan stalks off to sulk. Martyn stomps into the kitchen, and says

> "He is SUCH a prick. When
> does school start back? Why in
> the hell does he have so long off
> at Easter?"

before stomping back out.

Just gonna stay in the kitchen, bloating. It seems safer.

THE TOOTH FAIRY IS A LOAD OF RUBBISH

I got a phone call from school today. Brendan has *'sustained a head injury,'* and has *'an extremely wobbly tooth.'* I asked if he was OK. *'Oh, yes—of course! We put a cold compress on his tooth.'* I asked if it was the one that was wobbly already; the secretary was rather affronted, and seemed to feel that I wasn't being properly maternal and solicitous. *'Yes. He mentioned that it was loose before, when he came into the office from class.'* She didn't know how he had *'sustained'* the injury, but I felt certain that Bren would fill me in, in excruciating detail, when I collected him from After School Club.

Martyn collected the boys, and when I got home, Brendan came rushing to show me the hole where his tooth had been. It

> *"fell out totally during lunch, and a teacher just put it in my sandwich bag, since her office was really far away."*

I asked him what or whom he'd bumped into; he looked a bit embarrassed.

> *"Um, well, I was jumping in the air, right, because I was doing a flying sit-spin to get on the carpet, and I accidentally kneed myself in the face."*

Tristan was indignant.

> *"Why would school call you because Brendan is a dork?"*

Brendan smugly replied that Tristan was

> *"only just jealous, because I'm*
> *gonna put this tooth under my*
> *pillow and earn some money*
> *from the Tooth Fairy."*

Tristan snarls that he doesn't believe in the Tooth Fairy,
because

> *"she's just rubbish and*
> *not real, and who cares,*
> *anyway?"*

Brendan, scenting jealousy, goes for the withering put-down:

> *'Keep not believing in her,*
> *and YOU won't get ANY*
> *money. I keep believing in*
> *her, even though she's*
> *imaginary, because I love*
> *money."*

Belief is worth something, as it turns out: 25p.

GOOLY HOOLY MONSTER

*"Wow! That is a good picture. I'm
assuming it is a boy monster—doesn't
look like it has lipstick or long
eyelashes. Does it have a name?"*

[Exasperation. Withering scorn. Etcetera.]

*"MOM. Don't be ridiculous. I would
never draw a girl monster. Too stupid.
It has a species name: Gooly Hooly
Monster. A bit like a Gila monster,
which you said is pronounced 'heela'.
I'm glad you mentioned that when
Brendan wasn't paying attention.
Actually, he doesn't pay much
attention about science things anyway.
Do you want to know all about the
Hooly Monster?"*

*"Yep. Does he have magical or
non-magical powers? And what
are his powers?"*

*"Non-magical but deadly
'abilities', not 'powers'. It sounds
more serious to say 'abilities'. He is
venomous. He mostly kinda hangs
around in his lair, waiting for stuff
to get lured in there, because it
smells good in his lair. And then…*

...WHAM, he chomps them,
squirts poison with his fangs, the
poison goes in their veins... THEN
the blood comes out of their veins,
and he drinks it. He doesn't eat
their flesh right away; he saves that
for a snack before his bed-time."

Sometimes I am glad that the only dangerous creatures around here are boys. Their lair smells terrible, and I go into it as infrequently as possible.

SQUISHING AND PLOPPING

"Mom, how old were you when
you did your first time of cooking?"

"It was before I was 5, T. I used
to help with cooking a lot, just
like you do."

"Did you like licking the beaters
from the mixer as much as me?"

"Yep, think so. And I didn't get
to do as much beater-licking as
you do, because I had more
brothers and a sister."

"Do the people who are coming to
our house tomorrow when I'm at
school like licking beaters?"

"I would think so. I think most
people like to do it. I also think
some people don't do much baking,
and some people might not lick
beaters because they think it is silly
and not very proper."

"THAT would be sad, Mom. I
don't want to EVER worry that
much about properness. Do these
people not know about squishing
and plopping, either?"

"I'll bet they don't call it that, Tristan. They might never have gotten to push cookie dough off a spoon with their fingers before, so I think it will be fun for them."

"Adults worry too much about doing things the right way, and not enough about having fun. I think Dad can teach them to act like dorks pretty quickly, though, 'cause he is really good at it."

FATAL DISTRACTION

"Mom, were you always
distracted to guys with nearly
black hair and nearly black
beards?"

"Mart—Tristan wants
to know if I was
'distracted' to you."

"He didn't say distracted.
He said 'attracted.'"

"No I didn't! I said 'distracted'.
And were you, Mom? Ones with
brown eyes, and lots of eyelashes,
and jeans, and purple jumpers
and…"

Martyn interrupts with a smirk, pulling up his boxers. I
point this out to Tristan, who is still adding items to the
'distracted' list.

"Yeah, Mom, and boxers.
Did you always get distracted
by boxers?"

"I don't know, but I think Dad is
going to distract himself with a
wedgie. And I am definitely not
attracted to people having wedgies.
Their faces go all weird."

They don't hear me; they are in the Dad & Tristan equivalent of Brother Zone, and it has many of the same parameters as Brother Zone. Nothing is as funny as farting or a good wedgie joke.

> *"Ha ha hah ha ha! Dad! Pull harder on your elastics! You'll give yourself an AWESOME wedgie! Are wedgies sexy?"*

Snorting, giggling, and what should be an embarrassed Dad, who is actually quite shameless: there is nothing better. We are headed for a low-brow afternoon.

IT ISN'T SWEARING

"Holy Tish!"

Tristan chants repetitively, as Brendan smirks.

"Holy Tish!"

I hear it again, this time followed by lots of giggling and splashing. Finally, louder still,

"HOLY TISH! HOLY
TISH! HOLY TISH!"

I am tired and befuddled, thinking about a thousand different things, including a really annoying girl from primary school who was called *'Tish',* short for Patricia. He doesn't know anyone named Patricia, does he? I wonder.

"Holy Tish! It isn't swearing. It is
'shit' backwards, Mom, but I
won't say 'shit' again, 'cause that
is definitely swearing. HOLY
TISH, Brendan! Holy Tish!"

For the third time today, I wonder who this evil child is.

MY MOM IS NOT A MUMMY

> *"Mummy! OOOOOH*
> *WOOOOOOOOOoooooh.*
> *WooooooOOOOOOOOOoooh!*
> *You mean like on Scooby Doo?*
> *That is totally NOT what I call*
> *her. Don't call her that."*

Although

> *"Halloween is the best*
> *holiday, and only one day*
> *before my birthday, I don't*
> *like it if people call you*
> *'Mummy'. That is just too*
> *weird."*

Tristan has very firm ideas about what I should be called. He doesn't like it if people refer to me as *'Mummy'*. I have explained that it is pretty common for people in the UK to call mothers 'mummies'. I would prefer that they use my name, but that seems to be something many teachers and adults who work with kids refuse to do. Why, I have no idea. I REALLY don't like being called *'Mummy'*. It isn't a name that exists in my culture of origin, and I have never used it to refer to myself, unless I have been dressed like, well, a mummy of the Scooby Doo variety. It is also a word that I associate with toffs (though I have heard a lot of them say *'Mumsy'* instead, which is just...twee) and my Mother-in-Law. It is what she prefers to be called. And getting called the same thing that she wants to be called would just be tooooooooo weird.

Brendan drew a picture of a Mummy. The horror movie
kind—not me. It has beautiful, very sad, dark eyes.
Brendan said he knew that I wouldn't think that it was me,

> *"because YOU have blue eyes,*
> *and these are black. You also*
> *don't have a strange symbol*
> *like a railroad crossing sign*
> *on your forehead."*

It is good to know that there are certain clues, like the
absence of linen wrappings and forehead symbols and
brown eyes, to alert the general public to the fact that I am
not a mummy or a Mummy. I am definitely a witch, and I
am recycling my green, warty rubber nose from last year.

WHY IS IT THAT…

> *"Why, when you are waiting for*
> *something that you really want to*
> *happen, it gets over with really, really,*
> *quickly?"*

Brendan is in a pensive mood. He is wondering why it is still such a long time until Christmas, and why it is an even longer time until his birthday.

> *"Do you remember when I was*
> *waiting to lose my first tooth for ages,*
> *and then it took hardly any time for*
> *the dentist to take out, after I worried*
> *about it for so long, and food got stuck*
> *underneath, and germs got stuck there*
> *as well?"*

Yes. I sigh, feeling irritated as hell all over again. I certainly DO remember that, Brendan, because you were a shrieking hysteric. I will never be able to forget it. I am emotionally scarred. I don't say this, of course; what I say is something a bit more like this:

> *"Yes, honey, I remember. You*
> *worried for ages, didn't you,*
> *and it was all ready to come*
> *out on its own anyway."*

> *"But Christmas and my birthday*
> *were over so fast. I don't understand*
> *that. I feel like I blink and…*

…POOF, things have happened
while I looked away for a second.
Like waiting to have a movie come
out when I've seen the trailer, and
lots of times the movies aren't as
good as I thought they would be.
Did you feel like that?"

"Yep. I sure did. And then I was sad when
things I had been waiting for were over so
fast, too, just like you."

STILL FATALLY DISTRACTED

Tristan is still annoyed because *'attracted'* and *'distracted'*

> *"sound nearly exactly the same, but*
> *you told me they don't mean the*
> *same, and that is even more*
> *annoyinger than Brendan's*
> *laughing."*

We are deep in the throes of half-term break, or Hatred
Holiday. Brendan and Tristan have spent most of the last
week irritating each other, having titanic arguments, and
making up. If they weren't brothers, it would look like a
love affair to observers. Romulus and Remus, Cain and
Abel: the flip side of love is hate, and nowhere is it more
evident than in my house.

> *"Tristan, I keep telling you that they*
> *don't mean the same thing because*
> *they don't. They are almost opposites;*
> *they are about the same thing, which*
> *is paying attention. If you are*
> *attracted to someone or something,*
> *you pay a lot of attention to that*
> *person or thing. If you are distracted*
> *by something, it is taking your*
> *attention away from other things."*

> *"So if I say the Dad Bearded*
> *Dragon at Butterfly World who is*
> *called Troy got distracted to Helen,*
> *the Mom Bearded Dragon,*

*and then they had sex and after
that some eggs, that wouldn't be
right, would it?"*

"*Nope. You've got this figured out, I think.*"

"*All I know is, 'attracted' sounds way
too sexy and gross. I think I would
prefer to be 'distracted' to girls. I want
to have a motorcycle and a fretless bass
guitar, not girlfriends.*"

I give up. For today, for 5 minutes, I give up. I can't even
muster the energy to tell him that a fretless and a motorbike
are pretty much guaranteed to attract potential girlfriends.

Is it bedtime yet?

TWO PACK, 4 PACK, SIX PACKS, A BELLY

Brendan wants to have a 6 pack. More accurately, a 4 pack; he wants 2 lines going up and down, and one going across—a bit like squares. It is his current obsession. He looks at the cover of Men's Health every time we go to Margiotta's. Brendan keeps checking to see if his abs have gotten any stronger, or any better defined, since the last time he checked (usually less than 15 minutes before). He is disgusted with himself this evening. He

> *"only has a 2 pack. How old*
> *do I have to be to have a 4*
> *pack, anyway?"*

Anyone out there have the answer? Inquiring 8 year old minds, who fear that they are perhaps less overtly manned up than they should be, want to know. And if they stand with their arms tensed, curved around their stomachs in the stereotypical muscle-man pose,

> *"will this help a 4*
> *pack to grow"?*

DON'T BE SO SEXY

Tristan did not want me to put lipgloss

> *"or even lip ANYTHING,*
> *even chaff stick,"*

on this morning. He is concerned that I might possibly,
vaguely, potentially be considered sexy. Which is obviously
bad. Apparently. Moms should be invisible, I guess, just to
be on the safe side. Unless, of course, I am doing something
like

> *"carrying my amplifier when*
> *I take my electric guitar to*
> *P2 for Show And Tell, or else*
> *if I am with you at Asda,*
> *and I get lost, then it is OK"*

if I

> *"accidentally look sexy, because*
> *then someone could find you*
> *when I need you."*

Glad to have been of use.

BUILDING AN AIRPLANE ISN'T THAT HARD

*"We are going to do it
this afternoon, Mom."*

Hmmmm. I don't remember promising to do anything in particular. Must ascertain what exactly has been promised, and at what time, so that I can warn Martyn.

*"Who is 'we', and what are
they going to be doing?"*

*"Making an electricity project. Dad
said we can. It is going to be a plane, a
really big one, but NOT big enough
for me or Brendan to get inside. Which
is OK, because I am not sure I think
Dad can make a plane that won't
crash. Do you know if he ever builded
a plane before, Mom?"*

*"I am sure he has. Not one big enough
for people, though. I wouldn't worry too
much, T, because even if the plane you
make crashes, I am sure you could take
the electricity project motor out and use
it in another plane."*

"Well,"

he says, eyebrows pulled together, looking dubious,

*"well, as long as Brendan is flying
it when it crashes, I guess that
would be OK."*

FARTING AND CHRISTMAS DECORATIONS

We were stuck in traffic for 3 days. I lied. It was 35 agonizing minutes. The sight of the recently installed giant Norwegian spruce on The Mound, and the lights all over Princes Street Gardens, and St. Andrew's Square, seems to have sent Brendan and Tristan over the edge into some dark pit of maleness.

Exhibit A:

> *"Tristan, what is that awful smell? Are you farting?"*

[Cue girly shrieking and squealing]

> *"Brendan! Of course not! That's just poisonous gas, leaking out of my eyes and nose and mouth, from my BRAIN, you big toilet-face!"*

[Howling and shrieking]

> *"Tristan! That is so awesome! Let's sing the Fart Song! Mamma Mia / I have diarrhoea / how, how, HOW can I convince you? Yeah, we were broken-hearted / on the day we farted / Mamma Mia! I have diarrhoea!"*

ARGH.

[More and more shrieking. And, also, farting]

> *"BRENDAN! You are the COOLEST.*
> *Hairy Diarrhoea / Mamma*
> *Mamma Mia, my, my, how can I*
> *disgust you? / YEAH, you were*
> *broken-hearted/ just only because we*
> *farted / how can I make you puke,*
> *my my, oh yeah, hairy diarrhoea!"*

I banged my head on the steering wheel, over and over, harder and harder. It did not help. I could still hear and smell them.

I HATE HIM LOADS

Brendan and Tristan are bickering today. Constantly. All things are worth fighting over. Someone, neither is confessing, turned the bath tap to Arctic. So no bath. They are now writing insults to each other on the shower door, as the glass has fogged up and neither of them wanted to take a shower. They are narrating the insults, after accusations of the writing being too messy to read were bandied about. The enraged bellowing is shredding my patience. Small sample:

[Brendan]

> *"What? I'm not a loser, and I'm rubbing you out! You wiener-brain doggy butt!"*

[Tristan]

> *"You dunghead! Come over in MY side of the shower, and you'll be dead! HEY MOM! Did you hear me? I did RHYMING, Mom! And also I think Brendan wrote 'whiner' instead of 'wiener'."*

I am sure everyone in a 300 meter radius can hear them. I am bracing myself to go back in there. Now, they are both giggling, and I'm not sure I want to know what they find so funny. They are, abruptly, in Brother Zone. I peek around the corner, and I see Brendan slobbering big gobbets of foam.

> *"He had a small drink of shampoo, Mom, and he totally looks like the beagle with rabies in Fantastic Mr. Fox. I love him sometimes."*

TRISTESSE

According to dictionary.com, which supplies me with one
odd word per day, 'tristful' means sorrowful, full of woe, or
morose. It is a very appropriate word around here. Tristan
has been tristful all week, and couldn't wait to get back to
school. Snow Days

> *"are a total waste of time, when*
> *you have no one to play with but*
> *your brother."*

He was disappointed today. Everything went wrong.
He carried a gigantic lump of copper reclaimed from
an old hard drive,

> *"which was completely heavy, and*
> *then there was no Show and Tell."*

He got a lot of homework, and heavy cloud cover meant that
drawing the phases of the moon for a week isn't happening for
a few days. He has to wear ribbons and a waistcoat in his
Nativity show, and only has one line. He is

> *"doing the part of a Polish boy, and*
> *I like Polish talking and bread, but*
> *why do Polish boys look like those*
> *stupid Morris dancer guys from*
> *Chitty Chitty Bang Bang?"*

And, worst of all, he

> *"got punched in the ear, and it*
> *hurt, and I think maybe people*

thought I cried. I don't like crying.
It makes me feel little and stupid."

I am tristful too; ear punching is just plain nasty, and I now have to try to get Tristan to wear ribbons in front of a large audience.

SOME WORDS SOUND LIKE THEY MEAN SOMETHING ELSE

The boys are snorting and giggling. The still-almost-toothless Brendan is spraying the table and the rest of us liberally with bread crumbs. Martyn absentmindedly wipes them off the table and keeps staring at his iPhone.

Martyn has just mentioned a development project in Glasgow called 'New Gorbals'. The Gorbals has a reputation as a dangerous place, one of the least healthy urban areas in Europe, with low life expectancy for all, but particularly for men. It has been called a slum, Glasgow's dumping ground, The Concrete Jungle, and worse. Like the word 'feminism', 'the Gorbals' has a lot of bad press to live down. To me, it suggests somewhere in need of a facelift, funding, some infrastructure, and some respect. To the boys, 'the Gorbals' suggests something else entirely.

With even more giggling and snorting, they quickly move on to threatening to kick each other right in the Gorbals, while moaning and writhing in their seats, clutching their *tender Gorbals*. Can't take these two anywhere, probably not even the legendary Gorbals of the 1970s.

WE EAT WEIRD FOOD, MOM

*"Mom, why don't you ever get
me torpittas any more?"*

I have to think for a minute. Ah—got it.

*"Do you mean tortillas
or pitta bread?"*

*"The round circley yellow ones,
Mom. Like I said: torpittas!"*

*"They are made from corn,
which is why they are yellow,
and they are called 'tortillas'.
Will we put them on the
grocery list?"*

*"Nah. You can do it. I'm only 6,
and I don't think I can spell
'tortillas', because that isn't a
Scottish word."*

THE RETURN OF BREAD MAN

They were prepared. Camouflage wellies? Check. Stage
whisper & sniggering mode? Enabled.

> *'Do you think he's*
> *gonna be there again,*
> *Brendan? What will we*
> *do to him??"*

[Me]

> *"You won't do anything to*
> *him! Just leave him alone, get*
> *the bread, use your hands if*
> *you have to, and we'll get out*
> *of here."*

[Brendan]

> *"Describe him for me."*

[Tristan]

> *"He looks dorky. Old. Smelly,*
> *like old trainers. White hair.*
> *Dorky blue pocket raincoat.*
> *And...that's him!! There,*
> *Brendan!"*

They are now in Brother Zone: united in a secret world
where grownups are irrelevant, and things Mom says
bounce right off the forcefield. I tell them not to run; they
shuffle off at breakneck speed, wellies squealing on the
linoleum. Valvona and Crolla staff gasp in alarm, and fling
themselves out of the way.

Brendan and Tristan walk slowly along behind unsuspecting Bread Man, snorting with mirth, planning their attack. Bread Man is unaware that he is being stalked, past tomatoes and overpriced pasta. He's not after bread. He is, today, Cheese Man, and demands that staff fill his backpack with cheese, which he promises to pay for at the counter.

"Riiight,"

drawls Tristan. The girl behind the counter looks anxiously at me, wondering if I know something. I distract the vigilantes;

*"look, guys, the
samples are out!"*

They run, shrieking. Cheese Man hurriedly shuffles off. Tristan proudly uses the tongs to get the right bread

*"before Cheese Man
gets here."*

He and Brendan reminisce about their victory, and talk all the way home about how weird grownups are.

A word of warning, Cheese Man: neither of them believes you've paid for all of your cheese. They will be watching you closely.

BREATHTAKING

> *"Breathtaking. This hill is*
> *breathtaking, Mom."*

Tristan puffs to a halt, and leans against me. I hug him; there isn't anything else I can do. It isn't the hill that is breathtaking: it is his asthma. Martyn explains what 'breathtaking' actually means, and Tristan agrees that the view from Arthur's Seat at night, with snow falling on and around us, is

> *"Dad's sort of*
> *breathtaking as well."*

But he also thinks it is

> *"kind of stupid. It doesn't mean*
> *the right thing. Why do*
> *grownups say it when there are*
> *better words, like 'beautiful' or*
> *'stormy' or 'mountainy'? I*
> *thought lots of people must have*
> *asthma, like me."*

Tristan has always loved playing with words and

> *"making them fit better,"*

as he puts it. When he was two, he overheard me hissing that I was so annoyed I wanted to kill Brendan with my bare hands. (I didn't do it, by the way. Brendan didn't need to squeeze every loaf of bread in Tesco, but still does so, now and again, 3 years later). I said *'bare hands'*. Tristan heard *'bear hands'*.

The next day, I found him snarling by the toy box, hands curled into claws, offering to kill Brendan with

> *"my bear hands, if you*
> *don't put Buzz Lightyear*
> *down NOW."*

A warning growl, with paws extended, is now family shorthand for *'you are so dead when we get home / I get bigger / Mom isn't looking'*.

INDEX

Mary F McDonough grew up in the US, where after rigorous initiation ceremonies involving being force-fed raisins, she became an honorary boy. She was then allowed to watch her many, practically feral, male cousins and brothers dare each other to pee on electric fences, blow up G.I. Joe dolls, and ride mopeds at high speed through cow pats.

These early experiences prepared her well for being a *'Boy Mom'*, which she considers to be the next best thing to being a boy. She wants it to be clear, however, that she loves being a woman, and wearing corsets.

Mary is a communication consultant, therapist and writer.

www.maryfmcdonough.com

Martyn Clark grew up in and around farms in Ireland and Switzerland, eating mud pies, building hay forts, crashing tractors into outbuildings, and getting breeze blocks thrown on his head by his cousins. He somehow got distracted and confused by studying Physics and Singing, and trying to be a proper adult with a job.

Martyn always wanted to be a *'Girl Dad'*, so was surprised to discover that he had boys. He has since rediscovered the joys of playing conkers, hitting and burning things, making dens, and generally destroying stuff, while also learning to appreciate dancing and yoga.

Martyn is a musician, executive coach, and creative communication consultant.

www.martynclark.com

GADFLY

www.gadflyeditions.com